FEDOSKINO
ФЕДОСКИНО

Moscow
Izobrazitelnoye Iskusstvo Publishers
Москва
„Изобразительное искусство“
1990

ББК 85.12
Ф 33

Text and selection by
Nikolai Malakhov

Translated into English by
Tatyana Butkova

Designed by Alexander Zazykin

Photography by Yuri and Oleg Grigorov

Автор вступительной статьи и составитель
Н. Я. Малахов
Перевод на английский язык Т.Л. Бутковой
Художник А. И. Зазыкин
Фотографы Ю. Г. Григоров, О. Ю. Григоров

ф $\frac{4904000000 - 135}{024 (01) - 90}$ 90-без объявления

ISBN 5-85200-183-x

Fedoskino, an old village thirty kilometres off Moscow, sprawls on the bank of the Ucha river. The vistas opening from it are a feast for the eye, with green fields, silvery birch copses and the rich velvety green of pinewoods — the archetypal Central Russian landscape.

From the late 18th century, this landtilling village has been one of the most renowned seats of a refined handicraft, lacquer miniature painting on papier-mâché.

Lacquer painting on wood emerged in Russia in the first half of the 18th century. I.N. Ukhanova's book quotes interesting information on the initial stage of Russian lacquerwork, with ample references to sources which N.I. Arkhipov unearthed from archives and studied for the Petershoff restoration programme. As the artist restorers got busy with the badly damaged panels in the Chinese room of the Monplaisir palace of Peter the Great, they were amazed to see that these were of limewood, never used in China nor Japan, but the most conventional material for Russian artist-craftsmen. The fact found explanation in the documents found by Arkhipov. Among them was a contract of June 1720 with "a team of ten painters headed by journeymen Ivan Tikhanov and Perfili Fedorov and apprentices Ivan Polyakov and Ivan Nikiforov, working for the Admiralty" for "gilt lacquerwork, Chinese-style, in a room in Petershoff". Ninety-four panels brilliantly imitating Chinese work were ready by February 1722 to be installed in Monplaisir in October. "The imitation was so subtle that the later generations of artists and experts never had a shade of doubt that it was the real thing" (1).

The 18th-century Urals factories amply produced brass and iron kitchenware with lacquered ornamentations. Academician Pallas, who led a 1770 Academic expedition to the Urals, left in his report a passage full of admiration with these beautiful items manufactured at the Demidov factories in Nevya and Nizhni Tagil. He described it as an exquisite craft "in which the locals truly excel. They cover with lacquer painting brass and iron kettles, wooden bowls, glasses and trays" (2). The scholar also pointed out the rare durability of such vessels.

The considerable experience of the 18th century and the spreading popularity of lacquerwork resulted in lacquerpainting workshops opening throughout Russia. At the turn of the 19th century, the Moscow and St. Petersburg provinces each had a dozen minor factories producing papier-mâché snuffboxes and trays, and tinplateware. The Vishnyakov brothers, Filipp and Taras, gifted and enterprising serfs who bought their freedom, started a firm with branches in Moscow and Zhostovo village in its environs, which won renown in no time. In 1815, Yegor Vishnyakov started a business of his own in Ostashkovo village. The Novosiltsevo and Sorokino villages near Zhostovo soon had workshops of their own.

The leading enterprise belonged to the Korobov-Lukutin clan. It developed out of a small workshop started by the merchant Pyotr Korobov in 1795 in Danilkovo, an estate near Moscow. The exquisite handicraft caught his fancy when he visited the Stobwasser factory in Braunschweig, Germany, on his West European journey. With a good eye for business and an artistic flair, the merchant saw the great prospects of lacquer painting. He purchased a batch of paints and lacquers enough to start a business of his own from Herr Stobwasser and hired several artists-craftsmen from his factory. They quickly found gifted freemen in the surrounding villages to teach them, and the business took a promising start. Apart from the round painted snuffboxes quickly spreading throughout Russia to be known as "Korobov boxes", the factory produced lacquered peaks for army shakos.

At first, the Danilkovo men did not paint their boxes but decorated them with lacquered transfer-printed portraits of Russian statesmen and pictures from history. Preference was made from the most spectacular episodes of the Napoleonic war of 1812. Yet the first painted snuffboxes appeared even in Korobov's lifetime.

In 1818, a year before his death, Korobov passed the factory management to Pyotr Lukutin, his son-in-law (1784-1863). The business now flourished with a great assortment of produce: cigarette-cases, caskets, boxes for jewels, matches and powder, and chessboards. Their festive beauty went hand in hand with utility — suffice it to mention the travelling sets of papier-mâché wineglasses, one smaller than the other, the biggest holding the whole set. Several delightful samples are now on display at the Hermitage, Leningrad, and Moscow's History Museum.

A man of taste and seething energy, Lukutin had the make of a prosperous entrepreneur. A mere five years after he took over the business, the number of painters well exceeded fifty, the factory school teaching twenty apprentices at a time. In 1828, a royal edict gave the flourishing factory a trademark: Russia's coat-of-arms with Lukutin's full name or initials below.

Apart from precious and unique artefacts sold at exorbitant prices, the Lukutin factory mass-produced kitsch (3). The former, original works or copies from great paintings, were intended for aristocrats and the wealthiest businessmen. These were up to the tastes of the best-educated Russians, and took up all subjects to be found in the Russian and Western art: sophisticated allegories, scenes from the antiquity and modern history, genre, still-lifes, portraits — everything. To quote A.V. Bakushinsky, they "reflected the predominant artistic style of the time, with the opposing influences of Classicism and Romanticism, and the emergent realistic trends, all fantastically interlaced" (4).

The stuff intended for well-to-do peasants, the simple townsfolk, the impoverished nobility, clerks and small trading families went for a song. It was cheap stuff in every respect, of inferior techniques, with a sugary idyllic air. The thematic range of its genre scenes included folk festivals, prettified pictures of farmwork, dressed-up lasses posing by hedges, tender mothers, solemn greybeards, dashing troikas and ceremonious teaparties.

Mass-production did not bring down the artistic standards of the Lukutin factory. Oriented from the first on the best samples of Russian easel painting, with its wisdom and democratic tradition, it had an air of dynamism and artistic daring. In the first half of the 19th century, the Venetsianov school, with its power of observation and affinity with the people, was the dominating influence. Hence the inimitable style of Lukutin miniatures.

The period between the 1820s and 50s saw the factory turn to a profoundly understood Russianness. A trend all its own was emerging. Bakushinsky notes realistic principles pronounced in it. Naturally, the Lukutin miniaturists later sided with the *peredvizhniki* painters.

With all sentimental embellishment of life at the grassroots, the Lukutin painters were never alien to psychological insight. The truth of manner and character is always there — like in the *Peasant Dance* album cover miniature. Yet this psychological treatment always follows a limited set of patterns: dancers are always dashing, talkers full of well-wishing. Like the festive costumes, the well-fed, benign faces have little in common with serfs' life the way it really was.

Take the miniature depicting haymakers' rest: two pretty girls are reclining in the shadow of a tree, another two stand near them. Another group of four is resting at the wattlefence. The spick-and-span clothes, starched blouses and flimsy shoes — nothing but the rakes in two girls' hands reminds of the hard day's work. The exquisite chiaroscuro of the foreground and the misty vistas in the backdrops, with rows of haystacks opening in the perspective, add to the pastoral charm of the scene. Or another miniature, of peasants listening to a balalaika-player in a cosy veranda. With its penetrating, dreamland romanticism, the picture is a remote echo of the Italian Renaissance, an ideal of quiet, unattainable beauty in idealized but well-known Russian surroundings. Or take the cigar-box with a scene of courting, full of sad irony — the poor lass with the broom can hardly dream of a better fate than being the fat philanderer's plaything.

All this graceful sentimentality is not so naive as it may seem — there is a clash of a Dostoyevskian profundity between life-as-it-should-be, represented in these cloudless scenes, and life-as-it-was, which the painters knew all too well: they belonged to the limitless number of the humiliated and the insulted.

In his definition of the "realistically decorative quality" of the Lukutin miniatures, Bakushinsky combines both these contrasting qualities. Focusing his analysis on its informative value, he traces down the Venetsianov school influence on lacquer painting. "In this branch of the Lukutin miniature, we see a broader, more liberal treatment of copying", he writes. "The subject-matter is bravely reinterpreted 〈...〉 There are many original compositions. Surely, the serf painters could not realistically portray peasants, with their dependence on the oppressors they served 〈...〉 The pastoral idyll they depicted was, in fact, peasant life as seen from the nobleman's estate. The slaves' tragedy was hidden by the glowing colours of the miniatures. They graphically differed in style from the primitivism of the folk pictorial arts, with their one-dimensional, highly conventionalized decorative quality. What we see here is painting of the natural school, with its concentration on genre, three-dimensional representation acquiring a sculptural quality against the jet-black lacquer background. These miniatures show a rare power of observation and have many striking realistic features" (5).

Under Pyotr Lukutin, Russian miniature painting attained great artistic heights, with daring innovation in the subject-matter and decor. But true artistic perfection appeared when Alexander Lukutin joined his father as factory manager (1841-1863). The business had no rivals in Russia and equalled the gems of French and German lacquer miniature painting. Even the best samples were not so expensive as Western, which added to their popularity. The techniques reached such sophistication that even British masters borrowed knowhow from the Lukutin firm.

Two oil-painting techniques had taken shape as the dominant by that time, termed the solid and the airy. Done in thick impasto, the first required filigree details and a three-dimensional effect of an almost sculptural quality. Its rich local colours, however, often went together with a pearly transparency and refinement.

The other, "airy" technique used glazes: the greens of an underwater world, radiant reds and sunny yellows. Superimposed in several layers on mother-of-pearl plaques, goldleaf or aluminum powder rubbed with cotton wool into the varnished surface, they produced a luminous effect. Often combined with the solid local colours of direct painting, they were refined and festive.

The lids were often framed in metal or mother-of-pearl inlays. The sides were similarly decorated or had filigree plates of gold and silver imposed on them, in keeping with the late 19th century filigree vogue. Many articles were decorated with goldleaf, patterns embossed on it and covered in asphaltum varnish, the gold shining against its black gloss. Many snuffboxes were painted inside and outside in imitation tortoise-shell, birchbark, mother-of-pearl, mahogany or tartan. Combined, these decoration techniques achieved fantastic effects.

But let us not forget that papier-mâché was literally at the bottom of all this beauty. Its name literally translates from the French as chewed paper. Cheap and rather simple in manufacture, it has excellent plasticity and is as strong as the most solid kinds of timber. It is made of cardboard cut into stripes which are pasted together in several layers and dried in special chambers, the heat reaching 90 to 100 degrees centigrade. The produce resembles timber enough to be carpentered. Fresh from cabinet-makers, the semi-produced articles are puttied, primed with black and heat-dried once more. At last they are polished, coated in three layers of black varnish and vermilion, polished again, and varnished in transparent lacquer. At last, the boxes and panels are ready to be painted.

This technique had a long standing when the craft reached its peak. Lukutin articles had lots of gold medals from all Russian shows. They were exported on a large scale to Britain, Sweden, Germany and later America.

After his father died in 1863, Alexander Lukutin (1819-1888) became the sole master of the family business. It prospered as never before, with up to six thousand articles produced every year to the sum exceeding 23 thousand roubles.

Russian ethnic and social awareness burgeoned with the abolition of serfdom. It found reflection in the art of the second half-century, especially in *peredvizhniki* (Itinerant Art Show Society). The desire to bring the unadulterated truth into the portrayal of life at the grassroots swept the Lukutin miniature painters, too. "The easel painting of the 1860s-90s, brilliantly represented in the Tretyakov Gallery, was now the decisive influence on the Lukutin workshop to reflect the tastes of specific social groups, in particular, radically-minded intellectuals and other liberals. The Russian art of the 1860s and 70s, freshly after the Reform, abounded in naturalistic representations of peasant life in all its misery and crudeness. The Lukutin art was no exception. Perov, Maximov, Orlov and Myasoyedov, and later Repin, were amply copied," writes Bakushinsky (6). The Lukutin miniature thus remained democratically realistic, emulating easel painting, in its genre richness.

The Lukutin enterprise knew no rival up to the two closing decades of the 19th century. It ruined all petty competitors in the environs. In 1876 or somewhat earlier, Mr. Lukutin, Sr., promoted his son Nikolai to junior partnership. After his demise, in 1888, Nikolai became the sole owner of the family business of three generations and headed it till his death.

Nikolai Lukutin (1853-1902) had no makings of a big-time entrepreneur in him. Neither had he any interest in lacquer miniatures — or in medicine, for that matter, despite his education. A dedicated patron of the arts, he was Director of the Moscow Philharmonic Society and gave himself heart and soul to charity as sponsor of many institutions. His turbulent nature found no satisfaction in running the Fedoskino workshops. He thought lacquer painting outdated and not high-class enough for his ambitions. Stewards ran the business in between his rare visits.

The production was quickly losing its merits, turning into a mere handicraft producing sugary, low-taste artefacts by the hundred. Even the shapes lost their exquisite proportions for crudity and big sizes. More pretentious with every passing day, the Fedoskino articles shed their precious "sensuous feeling for the material world," to quote Bakushinsky. The spontaneous philosophical profundity was gone. The industry was evidently on the decline.

After Nikolai Lukutin died, the widow headed the business for two years, relying, like him, on thievish stewards. In 1904, the workshops were closed and the painters left to the mercy of fate. Some found employment in the primitive, stuffy Vishnyakov shop nearby — among them the gifted Kruglikov and Borodkin father and son. Others made do with chance earnings, painting inn and shop signs.

Yet the business got a new lease of life in autumn 1910. Keeping the secret from Vishnyakov, now a formidable competitor, six painters and four box-makers mortgaged all their possessions to start cooperative production in Semenischevo village near Fedoskino (7) — a genuine artistic commune run by an elective president. The cooperative met the Socialist Revolution of 1917 as a prosperous enterprise, up to its new tasks.

A retrospect of the over 100 pre-revolutionary years of Fedoskino painting shows that it had travelled a truly heroic way. With capitalist commercial interests often running counter to the truth and beauty of art, with no education and open to lots of mutually contradictory artistic influences, the painters always remained faithful to realism and preserved their refined techniques.

They borrowed on the classics of easel painting, with masterly chiaroscuro, precise line, and fine brushstroke — the best techniques for lacquer miniatures. Many art historians appreciated it. To quote G. Yalovenko, "Brought up on the best realistic traditions, the Fedoskino cooperative painters allowed grassroots realism to survive. They preserved the customs of the trade, the unique techniques and their high standards" (8). "The last of the Mohicans," as Bakushinsky described them, the artists carried on the Lukutin heritage of Russian realistic miniature painting.

Let us now analyse their aesthetics and impact on Russian art as a whole.

Says Yalovenko: "The Lukutin lacquer articles belong to the applied arts. Like other decorative articles of everyday use, they are not dominated by painted images but are seen as graceful wholes, beautiful and utilitarian at once'' (9). In other words, a snuffbox representing Peter the Great or the heart-rending picture of a famous shipwreck is on a par with an enamel plate or a painted tray.

Says Ukhanova: "Miniature copies of easel paintings represented negative influences as distracting the artists' minds from their basic task, making pretty and practical things" (10).

Many art scholars side with this view — which we, however, see as prejudiced or, at least, one-sided. Fedoskino miniatures tended to genre from the start, the artists drawing inspiration in easel paintings, book engravings and folk prints — hence the widely current portraiture of historical personages, everyday life scenes and landscapes.

The Hermitage Museum preserves several articles, among them a snuffbox inlaid with tin on the inside, with a breast portrait of Peter the Great in a green coat on the lid. Another, gracefully elongated box, represents a dashing troika. The driver, in a vermillion shirt and blue coat, never minds the galloping horses — he is lost in talk with his two fair passengers. Judging by the girls' countenances, he must be saying risky things. Two other snuffboxes, approximately similar in size, are round. One represents a young lady playing the lute, the other an old jeweller in a red neckerchief, weighing a heavy gold chain in his hands. The artistic techniques are evidently in the foreground in all these articles, disproving the utilitarian concept of the Fedoskino miniature.

Many boxes were decorated with Moscow landscapes. The Cathedral of Basil the Blessed, Red Square and the Kremlin embankment of the Moskva were often represented. The Fedoskino Museum boasts a box depicting the Kremlin as seen from across the Moskva River, with the bridge silhouetted against the sky — a graceful foreground to the crenellated outlines of the walls, the towers, church cupolas and the majestic belltower, all gossamer in the amber light of the setting sun, with an exquisite perspective in the best traditions of easel painting. Another miniature of the same period depicts Red Square seen from the History Museum, dominated by the Cathedral of Basil the Blessed and the Spassky Tower, a glorious background for the Minin and Pozharsky statue and the surrounding edifices. The refined landscape is merrily contrasted by the naively executed human figures: fine ladies and foppish carriage drivers. The composition and colour scheme richly draw on easel painting. A similar trend is seen in the St. Petersburg landscapes, evident imitations of Fyodor Alexeyev.

Importantly, the variety of snuffbox shapes does not allow us to judge which is the most convenient. With the amazing variety of pictorial metier, it is hardly possible to conclude that "they bring out the decorative and utilitarian quality" (11). Besides, one and the same landscape or genre scene is often met on a snuffbox, jewel box and casket. Take the snuffbox with the portrait of Countess Elizabeth Vorontsoff. The image of a society beauty lost in sad meditation is, surely, more important than the snuffbox itself — unlike in purely decorative articles in everyday use.

The miniatures were hardly meant only to emphasise the shapes. We doubt the conventional viewpoint on miniatures as sheer decor, whatever the Lukutins did to establish it, and later the local authorities and the Handicraft Museum custodians. It is high time to finish with the humiliating concept of Fedoskino miniatures as the ugly duckling among the fine arts. The paintings made the articles more than snuffboxes or caskets. The artists used utilitarian articles for their exquisite and profound realistic painting. Their style grew ever more sophisticated in colour scheme and composition — this latter entirely their own through richly drawing on easel pictures.

Many artists' names did not go down to us. They did not matter much at their time. The main thing was the trademark of their workshop. Now, we admire the powerful gift and perspicacity with which the miniaturists brought the patterns of easel painting to their art. The scenes are refined in their simplicity, precise in line and sophisticated in composition. The figures are three-dimensional, the colours festive, now emphasised by the mother-of-pearl or gold and silver inlays, now delicate and trasparent. Drawing in equal measures on the folk art, easel painting and engraving, miniature art was among the supreme acts of artistic creation. It was magnetically drawn to easel painting as the most complicated form of art. Even at the inception of the Lukutin period, this folk art transgressed the borders of grassroots decorative crafts and progressed toward professional art, not decoration.

True, the Lukutin painters were enticingly naive as they represented pastoral idylls. They even displayed lack of professionalism, with violated perspectives and proportions (for instance, their children look more like dwarfish adults) — typical features of folk art. Yet all are simple and wise stories of rural and urban life, folk customs and Nature. Hence the ethnographic interest in all social classes. These features of the Lukutin miniature were well described by art historian Gryaznov: "The pleiad of Russian painters of the 18th and 19th centuries is dear to us not only for their high professionalism but, even more so, for its encyclopaedic representation of Russian contemporaneity the way it really was. Likewise, the nameless Fedoskino masters left us no less precious testimony of life at the grassroots" (12). These works are nothing like-as-dust mass-produced things in everydays use. Everyone starts a dialogue between the painter and the owner. "No owner of a Fedoskino miniature will utilize the object which bears it — unless he has not the slightest respect for things of beauty. This is why the articles are never used," Gryaznov says later on (13). For a long time now, Fedoskino produces not only boxes but big plates of no utilitarian use, and large portraits made to order — none inferior in their psychological insights to the best easel portraits.

Clearly, papier-mâché miniatures exist on a par with murals and easel paintings, with realistic imagery of profound aesthetic content, top-class execution and exquisite colour schemes, and original line and composition. The decorative element enters only in their ornamental quality to tie the shape in with the painting. The Fedoskino miniature is an art, not craft — with a universe of imagery and a variety of genres. It includes portraiture, genre scenes, landscapes, Romantic pictures of revolutionary events and scenes from tales of magic. Even if it is the younger sister of easel painting, it is an equal member of the family.

The October 1917 Revolution opened a new page in the history of the Fedoskino cooperative. Even the early Soviet years demanded a dramatic increase of production. At that time, the enterprise had top-notch painters, among them V. Bolshakov, Z. Burbyshev, A. and I. Semyonov, N. Tsybin, K. Ranovsky, N. Petrov and V. Lavrov. At first, they remained true with traditional teaparties, troikas and scenes of home, sweet home.

Prior to the Revolution, the cooperative work was supervised by the regional authorities and experts from the Handicraft Museum. "The local authorities saw the miniaturists as mere craftsmen, not independent artists. So they were supposed to humbly make copies and adopt whatever artistic culture their betters chose to give them," wrote Bakushinsky (14). The situation survived onto the Soviet time. Early in the 1920s, the Handicraft Museum supplied the workshops with articles to be copied. All came from the brush of artists on the museum staff — a pushing lot hardly marked by genius. Their work left much to be desired and ran counter to the Fedoskino standards. At best, "they had to repeat motives predominant in the Soviet art of many trends — some bitterly opposed to each other. The view of them as sheer copyists always prevailed," says Bakushinsky (15), while "the task was to encourage their creative initiative" (16), proceeding from the trends in their art and Soviet cultural demands in general; to develop the realistic Lukutin school, "bringing it closer to the present-day situation" (17).

The Fedoskino artists could not easily overcome the inferiority complex they had developed when the enterprise was on the decline. That was why they clung to the traditional troikas, teaparties, folk dances and rural festivals, in which Tsybin excelled in the 1930s. Exquisite still-lifes by Platonov, the Semyonov brothers, Borokin and

Ranovsky were the first attempts to enlarge the thematic range — yet it was not enough in the era of sweeping social upheavals. Kruglikov, I. Semyonov, Borodkin, Lavrov and Petrov were the first to make the stride to contemporaneity.

I. Semyonov looks traditional enough in his 1934 miniature *Collective Farm Family at Tea*, with the conventional samovar and painted teapot, yet the woman looks typical for the 1930s, the countenances are individualized and the postures more spontaneous than the old pattern demanded.

Petrov's *Landscape with a Herd* (1936) was a real landmark in Fedoskino landscape painting. Executed in the transparent technique, of which he was the paragon, it presents a forest glade at sunset, with a cluster of oaks, lacy foliage against the golden sky, and the grass criss-crossed with the shadows of the mighty tree-trunks. In the foreground is a shepherd boy playing his pipe, two girls reclining nearby, backs resting against a tree stump, are lost in the sweet tune, forgetting about their baskets full of mushrooms. Cows are grazing near them — a simple picture but so full of *joie de vivre* and love of life, with its colours and all-penetrating poetry. It took a truly free artist to make it, an artist of frankness and thorough knowledge of both miniature and easel techniques. Petrov loved glowing colours: shining reds, emerald greens, and all shades of blue and yellow.

Multi-figure compositions were a rarity in the Fedoskino of the time, with new themes and no tradition of such compositions, four or five being the most in conventional miniatures.

In the 1930s, the dominant task was to copy Russian classics, like Pavel Fedotov and the Makovsky brothers, and foremost Soviet painters, Johannson, Gerasimov, Grekov and Bogorodsky among them. Again, easel painting was their starting point, with its colour schemes, compositions, chiaroscuro specifics, etc.

Not that the miniatures became sheer copies — neither the solid nor the airy techniques allowed it, with the traditional decorative quality and the black lacquer background. Yet we should not idealize the decorative quality as allegedly the backbone of miniature painting. Neither shall we shed tears because "copying pictures without their strict selection accounted for easel techniques moving into the front in miniature painting at the expense of its decorative element" (18).

In 1931, apprenticeship was renewed in Fedoskino after a thirty-year break when, at oldest masters' request, a vocational school was established with three and four year courses to train painters and modellers. By the early 1940s, among the graduates were the gifted G. Tochenov, M. Pashinin, V. Lipitsky, Z. Tsar, A. and I. Strakhov, M. Chizhov, S. Rogatov, R. Sedova, A. Parfenov, V. Korsakov, S. Tardasov and other excellent painters. Some later developed into leaders to determine the Fedoskino progress for the next two or three decades.

World War II accounted only for a several months' break, when the frontline was a dozen miles off the village. The Lukutin and later collections were safely hidden. Many painters joined the Army. Yet the work was soon revived thanks to the Russian Federation government decision of February 7, 1943, on encouraging folk arts and crafts, with the ensuing allocations.

Many wartime works deal with the war and other glorious military pages in Russian history, among them Kruglikov's *The Poltava Victory*, I. Semyonov's *Salute in Moscow*, and Popenov's portrait of Marshal Tolbukhin.

The workshop was fully revived with the postwar demobilisation of prominent artists who had finished the Fedoskino school shortly before the war: Pashinin, Lipitsky, Rogatov, Strakhov, P.N. and P.S. Davydov, and Orlov. One by one, memorable miniatures from recent war history appeared, among them Pashinin's *Victory Salute*, Lipitsky's *Heroism at the Front and in the Rear,* and P.N. Davydov's *Liberators*.

Traditional Lukutin subjects fruitfully survived beside them. Subjects from Russian tales, landscapes and still-lifes were prominent now, too. Sketches from nature resulted in many wonderful landscapes by Strakhov and Rogatov, made all the better with a touch of fantasy. Genre and portraiture are no less prominent — suffice it to mention the portraits of Pushkin and Lermontov by Pashinin and Lipitsky, the Lenin cycle, and P.S. Davydov's *Maxim Gorky on the Volga*. Many masters turned back to purely decorative Lukutin articles in imitation tartan, tortoise-shell, or filigree.

Genre, landscape, portrait, still-life, a historical painting — whatever a Fedoskino artist does, he makes it a point to present images permeated with the spirit of the time. This quality makes contemporary miniatures different from the Lukutin, with their naive pastorale air. Fedoskino keeps abreast of the entire Soviet art.

* * *

Now, you may ask who were the wonderful 19th-century painters. Regrettably, we know only a few names of the oldest cohort: F. Sklokin, S. Matveyev, and the two Shavrin brothers. Of great interest were S. Borodkin, with his troikas and tea parties, and D. Krylov of inimitably coloured landscapes and first-class copies of *peredvizhniki* paintings.

V. Borodkin, son of S. Borodkin, a top-notch painter, had his right arm amputated during World War I and with careful training developed his left hand enough to get back to the workshop. He created solid technique masterpieces: landscapes, still-lifes and genre scenes — mostly original interpretations of Russian and Western classics. His *Hunter and Sleeping Peasant Girl* quintessentially presents his manner.

A. Kruglikov, another of the founding fathers of the Fedoskino cooperative enterprise, equally excelled in the solid and airy techniques, sometimes combining them to a striking effect. He preferred troikas, dancing girls, tea parties, Moscow townscapes and rural landscapes — all lyrical and majestic at the same time. Now he showed girls in their Sunday best, dancing on a forest glade in the last, dark-golden rays of the setting sun, the glowing colour of their dresses painted against goldleaf making an exquisite play. In *The Coquette*, his brush is fine in the presentation of the face, hands, dress and jewels. You will hardly forget these joyful features. The miniature *Holiday-Makers* presents archetypal people of the 1930s: three men and five women, all dressed up, picnicking on a river bank with a samovar. The landscape merges with the festive scene.

V. Lavrov, who honourably represented the fourth generation of the Lavrov artistic family who had started with the Lukutins, was fine in the solid and airy techniques, preferring scenes of rural life, teaparties and portraits in the traditional manner. You can hardly tell his compositions and colour schemes from samples of a hundred years before his lifetime, with red and blue shirts, white aprons, with the same samovars, cups and sugar-basins, and repeating the same diagonal compositions. It was the way his great-grandfather, grandfather and father had painted. Now, Victor Lavrov and Nikolai Ivanov have been with the Fedoskino workshops for thirty-five years or so — the fifth Lavrov generation.

Yet don't think V. Lavrov only reverently imitated his ancestry — some of his teaparties are inimitable in colour and composition. He achieved masterly combinations of thick impasto and fine glaze, with amazing coloristic effects. Most of all he liked miniature copying of Pavel Fedotov and Karl Bryullov.

I. Semyonov, one of the leading Fedoskino artists in the prewar time and the 1940s, started his career in the Vishnyakov workshop. His gift flourished when he joined the Fedoskino cooperative. A painter of a wide thematic range, he excelled in genre scenes, portraits of Soviet leaders, landscapes and still-lifes. Many of his works depicted contemporary rural scenes, with a new treatment of traditional topics, like the rustic courting in *The Accordion-Player* or the farmwork in *Harvest*.

No usual is A. Leznov's work. An apprentice of Vishnyakov's, he worked in many artist craftsmen's teams near Moscow, including the Zhostovo tray production. Its gorgeous flower bunches and fantastic fruit went over to Fedoskino miniature thanks to him, with local colours daringly combined and fantastic floral arrangements against the black background, with the Zhostovo three-dimensional presentation always there, but the graphic line slightly mollified.

I. Platonov, another older-generation master, had preference for good old troikas and farm scenes (*Harvest, A Threshing-Floor, The Plowman,* and *Peasants*). He lavishly adorned his sophisticated compositions with gold patterns, which went together with the tans and yellows of the freshly plowed soil and ripe wheat.

M. Popenov stayed with the workshop for almost twenty five years, till the early 1950s. One of the best in the older generation, he was famous for the miniature copying of giant, tremendously difficult canvases by Surikov, Repin, Perov and Vasnetsov. His wartime copy of Vasnetsov's *The Three Bogatyr Knights* breathed patriotic inspiration. He did much to move miniatures still closer to easel painting. His independent works present him as an excellent genre painter. In *The Mowers,* he shows a man with a scythe and two women with rakes, going back after a busy day in the meadows. Accurately inscribed in the square of the casket lid, every figure has a countenance and posture like no other. The surrounding landscape is of rare refinement and precision of line.

Z. Tsar, one of the first women painters, graduated the Fedoskino school shortly before the war. The majority of her works are variations on well-known Russian paintings and traditional Fedoskino topics. Take one of her earliest works, *Frightened by a Snake,* from K. Trutovsky's original — a topic earlier taken up by I. Semyonov to produce quite a different effect. Tsar worked in impasto, with trees subtly outlined against the late afternoon sky, and spreading steppeland crossed by a river in the background. The snake across the path, and the human figures in their startled postures are full of expressive force. The young mother and little boy are three-dimensional with the fine play of colour and masterly chiaroscuro — a reminiscence of mid-19th century Russian painting. Tsar is no inferior in the airy technique with top class portraits, and genre and historical scenes.

More decorative are the works by D. Orlov, who started shortly before the war. His airy-technique fairy tale scenes and troikas are painted on mother-of-pearl plaques, often with silver and gold inlay. He displays rare taste in decoration, always harmonious with the miniatures. More often than not, the painting plays second fiddle to the decorations. Exquisite and artistic to the utmost, they represent the decorative trend in Fedoskino.

Tales and ballads inspire many artists to works full of feeling and festive in their intense colour. Like genre scenes, they are full of psychological insight, with legendary figures larger-than-life.

A. Kozlov's *The Tale of Tsar Saltan* and N. Babashko's *Fairy Tale* are done in complicated glazing techniques on goldleaf and varnished aluminum plaques — pioneer efforts in miniature painting. Luminous, precisely composed, with fine outlines, both are true things of beauty. The black lacquer framing of the colourful *Fairy Tale* adds to the effect.

Neither artist limits his work to tales and ballads. Kozlov painted portraits of Lenin, Dzerzhinsky, Gorky and Nikolai Ostrovsky, and compositions *The Panfilov Division* and *Military Parade. 1941.* In these last few years, he produced excellent landscapes: *March, April, Spring, Winter* and *Solowki Islands.* Babashko is the author of *Lenin as Little Boy, Lenin in St. Petersburg* and portraits of Nadezhda Krupskaya, Lenin's wife, and Zoya Kosmodemyanskaya, an undaunted guerrilla fighter in World War II.

S. Monashov also pays much attention to tales. The triumphant colours of his *Ivan Tsarevich and the Fire-Bird,* made in glazing, are emphasised by the non-traditional oval shape of the casket. The artist is well known for his topical *They Want Peace* and *Dancing* and portraits of Lenin and Bolshoi stars. Filigree on lacquer is his latest passion. Monashov invented many new burin shapes allowing to achieve an infinite variety of patterns on aluminum foil.

In love with decoration, S. Tardasov achieved a striking effect in his *Little Humpback Horse,* on a round plaque, with three bands of subtle gold-and-silver inlaid patterns, standing out against the black lacquer as reflections of the glowing colours in the central painting. Tardasov is also known for his compositions *Leningrad, Akhtyrka, Moscow Celebrates 800th Anniversary* and *Horses Watering*. He co-authored some works with Lipitsky, Pashinin and Rogatov.

Of landscapes, so prominent in the Fedoskino art, I. Strakhov was the best master. Permeated with lyricism, his pictures of Central Russia are based on sketches from nature. In *Tourists*, the shimmering background brings out the gossamer brushstrokes in which he portrayed the lush grass and foliage in the foreground. The *Riverscape* presents the moon rising over his native village, the lights lighting in the houses, the graceful old church standing out against the evening sky — a contrast to the glass-and-concrete house being built. The gilded river with a couple in a boat adds a human touch to the picture framed in the ruddy-greenish trees.

Strakhov knew no rival in the portrayal of spring, with its pearly flood water, and winter, with crystal snow. The sky is always different in his miniatures, emphasising the atmosphere of each. An unsurpassed master of perspective, he opens vistas up to the horizon. The black lacquer is always part of the general colour scheme, like in *The Village of Shushenskoye* or *The Village of Fedoskino*, bringing out the graceful silhouettes of trees and houses. Tiny details — foliage and grass blades, done in fine brushstrokes — do not divert our attention from the whole, framed in lacy gold inlay to remind us of canvases in gorgeous framing: testimony to Strakhov's rare eye for composition.

P.N. Davydov's *Pushkin's Winter Outing* presents the poet on a drive around his estate. He stands leaning on the sled, while the coachman trims the harness. The beautiful landscape imbues this simple scene with a poetic spirit. Among his historical miniatures are the superb *Leningrad* and *Vasili Chapaev*. No less catching is the humorous *Bear in a Sledge* (*General Bruin*).

Strakhov, Lipitsky, Pashinin, the Davydovs, Chizhov, Rogatov, Larishev, Karapaev, Tolstov, Antonov, Frolov and Puchkov opened a new page in the Fedoskino painting. Worthy successors to the older masters, they are now in their prime, many awarded honourable titles. At the turn of the 1950s, some of them were senior students of the Fedoskino vocational school, others freshly demobilized from the Army — all acutely feeling the local drive for artistic improvement and general erudition. From copying the community went over to independent works varying on the old themes: Russian tales, genre scenes and landscapes. The revolutionary history was also prominent, giving the world the glorious Fedoskino Leniniana.

V. Lipitsky was among the most prominent painters of the Lenin theme. His miniatures *To Visit Lenin, Lenin Walking, Lenin with Children* or *Lenin with a Newspaper* are emotional in their intense colour and austere line. In the latter miniature, we see Lenin looking through the latest Pravda issue. Majestic in his unassuming simplicity, this image is on a par with the best portraits of Lenin we know. Realistic like an easel painting, the work is still conventionalized in the Fedoskino way. Lipitsky pays much attention to folklore, suffice it to mention his *The Lady of the Copper Hill, A Scarlet Flower (Beauty and the Beast), The Royal Maiden, A Flower of Stone, Snow-Maiden, The Humpback Horse* and *Lel Sings*. The artist painted a gallery of Soviet and Western leaders' portraits. One noticeable miniature presents Pushkin composing verse — the vision of inspiration. Among his superb lanscapes, *Morning* and *An Evening in the Countryside* stand out. His genre paintings display a rich imagination: *A Girl Going for Water, An Evening Meeting, Leave-Taking, A Birch in the Meadow, This Old Waltz, An Evening near Moscow, A Shrovetide Scene* and *Pedlars,* to name but few. *A Scarlet Flower* shows Beauty, winning in her purity, clasping the magic flower to her breast, against the fantastic castle background framed in greenery. The black lacquer is functional here, symbolizing the mysterious air of the tale. Realistic, drawn from the grassroots, Lipitsky's works show a technical perfection based on the Lukutin traditions. The artist once transgressed the limits of miniature to paint his large panel *Unknown Soldier*.

I.
Fedoskino Factory of Lacquer Miniature Painting
Awarded with the Order of the Badge of Honour.
1982

II.
Artist Alexander Gerasimov visiting lacquer miniature painters at Fedoskino.
Standing, from left to right, G. Tochenov, M. Popenov, A. Novoselsky, A. Kruglikov;
seated, I. Platonov, A. Gerasimov, Z. Tsar.
1946

III.
Fedoskino lacquer miniature painters.
From left to right,
V. Nalimov, V. Lipitsky, M. Pashinin, M. Chizhov.
1982

IV.
P. Puchkov at work in his studio.
1982

V.
In the studio.
1982

VI.
Pupils of the Fedoskino School of Lacquer Miniature Painting
working in the open air.
1982

S. Rogatov excels in genre scenes, landscapes and still-lifes painted now in impasto, now in glaze on mother-of-pearl plaques or gold and silver leaf. He is unsurpassed in inscribing his intricate composition in ovals, octagons and circles. His *Georgian Dancer, Cattle Watering, Moscow Environs, Birch-Trees* and *Landscape with Partridges* are for years copied at the Fedoskino factory with slight changes. *Birch-Trees* shows his technical perfection and the creative use of the local landscape-painting patterns.

Over 200 miniatures belong to M. Pashinin, including the well-known *Lenin with Sverdlov, Lenin with Dzerzhinsky* and portraits of Lenin, Dzerzhinsky, Yesenin, Mayakovsky and Nikolai Ostrovsky. Of wide renown are his fairy-tale works: *Lel, A Flower of Stone, The Snow-Maiden* and *Lel and the Snow-Maiden*. The latter is marked for psychological insight into the legendary heroes portrayed against the archetypal Russian landscape. The boy's face shows love and inspiration, the girl's is full of sadness. The whole is a ballad in line and colours — melancholy and tuneful. The shadowy tree shapes in *Lel and The Snow-Maiden* let us feel the mysterious world from which these fantastic characters emerge. *Pushkin on the Neva Embankment* shows the poet among the cold pearly colours of the north.

M. Chizhov has preference for historical sites around Moscow (*Old Battle Site in Yakhroma*) and for beauty spots near Fedoskino. In *A Winter Scene in Zagorsk*, the good old troikas are painted against the monastery background, a bus standing out in a counterpoint of contemporaneity. The black lacquer clashes with the colourful buildings and the white snow, dark figures in the foreground taking off the sharpness of the contrast. *Winter Festivities in Fedoskino*, a multifigure composition inscribed in the circle of the round casket lid, makes the sled procession move in a curve to repeat the circular shape. The pearly *Winter Scene in Fedoskino* is typical of Chizhov in its lyricism. Sketches from nature made the basis of Kruglikov's, I. Semyonov's and other portraits. Chizhov greatly contributed to the Leniniana with his *Electric Lighting, Children Visiting Lenin* and other miniatures. He is drawn to heroic epics *(The Lay of Igor's Host)*, to revolutionary history *(Mayday, Red Army Raid)* and the history of World War II *(Liberation of Volokolamsk)*. Together with Korsakov, Tardasov and Monashov, the artist is working to revive the Lukutin techniques of filigree decoration and imitation tartan and tortoise-shell.

The vast thematic range of Fedoskino painting is well illustrated by A. Sokolov's *Leo Tolstoy*, A. Grachev's *Tula Smiths*, P. Macheyev's *Moscow Cityscape*, N. Balashov's *Landscape* and portraits of Suvorov and Marshal Zhukov, N. Aldoshkin's *Spinster*, G. Tochenov's *Troika*, M. Kornienko's *Evening Landscape* and V. Golenev's *Gramophone*.

G. Skripunov has been with the Fedoskino factory for over thirty years after graduation from Moscow's Applied Art College. His over 100 works treat now revolutionary history *(The Storm of the Winter Palace, October Revolution* and *The Battle of Kakhovka)*, now ancient epic subjects *(Prince Igor's Campaign, Yaroslavna's Lament)*, now athletic events *(Cross-Country Raid, The Finish Is Near!)*, now the beauty of Nature. *Winter Scene* shows an ancient Russian town with miserable little houses and majestic old edifices standing side-by-side. *Winter Festival* and *New Year's Eve* represent merry winter pastimes.

G. Larishev draws inspiration in all kinds of topics. Many of his 200 works are dedicated to Lenin, like *An Encounter* and *Electric Lighting* — both awarded gold medals. The impassioned pictures from revolutionary history are hauntingly Romantic: *The Year 1917, Machine-Gun Cart, For the Soviet Power,* the latter a hymn to the Red Army. Yet his attention is drawn even closer by the present day, with athletic activities (*New Town, Young Masters, Komsomols* and *A Horse-Race*), the space effort (*Our Gift to the Moon, Cosmos* and the fantastic *From Tale to Reality,* with a magic carpet among stars and constellations), and historical pictures from everyday life: *The First Radio-Set in the Village, Concert, The First Tractor* and *Successors.* Tragedy-laden are *Mother's Waiting Forever* an *An Old Woman Reading Her Late Husband's and Son's Letters.* In the first, an old woman, statuesque in her bereavement, stands near a gnarled tree, blind to the seething life around. In the second, an old woman looks through her family archive, lost in the reminiscences of a happy past. *Zhostovo Tray Painters* is original in composition and humorous in the portrayal of folk craftsmen. Or take the fairy-tale *Snow-Maiden*, with the villagers coming to say farewell to the charming presence. No one is left indifferent. Some talk away feverishly, others are on the verge of tears, yet others wave goodbye or stand stock-still with emotion. *Alyonushka* is remarkable for its mysterious landscape background. The golds and reds of *Autumn* show Larishev as an unsurpassed master of colours, with preference for reds and pinks contrasted with all shades of green.

L. Stroganova's *Lel* is no less remarkable, with mother-of-pearl inlays for the girl's dresses and gold for the foliage above, standing out against the locale colours of the painting. Executed in a different manner, her *Women Painters of Khokhloma* are no less decorative.

A. Tolstov painted many miniatures dedicated to Lenin: *Brothers, Lenin with Children, Lenin as a Child,* and *Lenin and Krupskaya in Gorki Village,* to name but few. Many works depict the rural contemporaneity, among them *My Village, At the Well, Winterscape, Return from Hay-Making, Winter Scene in the Countryside, Village Weekend, Wedding, Thaw,* and *Russian Dance. A Boy Reading a Letter to His Granny* resembles the traditional teaparty. Tolstov's genre scenes are multi-figured and festive in colour. *Evening Relaxation,* dominated by reds, is reminiscent of other works, like *Return from Hay-Making* or *My Village.* Even horses are painted in glowing red. This master is notable for a pronounced decorative quality going hand-in-hand with verisimilitude.

V. Frolov's *Tea-Drinking* is a present-day scene, with graphically individualized postures and countenances. The three dancing *Buffoons* are remarkable for precise composition and fine execution. The over fifty original works by Frolov include the top-class *Architect, Smithery, Pipers, Prince Igor Takes Leave of Yaroslavna, The Turkestan-Siberia Railway,* and *Rostov the Great.* Several works are dedicated to Lenin, among them *Lenin in October 1917* and *Lenin with H.G. Wells.*

P. Puchkov is remarkable for his cityscapes. *A View of the Kremlin* is decorative with street lights and the austere silhouettes of the Kremlin. *The Building of the Council of Ministers* lovingly depicts graceful bridges across the Moskva and the latest glass-and-concrete highrises, to which his brush gives a majestic air. In *Zaryadye in Moscow,* the artist shows an exquisite church ensemble dominated by the Cathedral of Basil the Blessed. The emphasis on architectural details does not diminish the decorative beauty of his works. Puchkov contributed to Leniniana with his *Lenin and Krupskaya in Gorki* and *Gorki Village.*

Y. Gusev, with his love for decoration, is a pupil of Lipitsky, Pashinin and Chizhov, with a pronounced influence of the renowned ornamentalist Tardasov. In the 1950s, he painted his casket *Lady onto Lassie,* the plaques *Fortieth Anniversary of the October Revolution* and *Roads in Moscow Environs* and many patterned boxes. His greatly-varied shapes go together with the paintings. Gilt floral patterns with mother-of-pearl inlays are his trademark. Gusev has lately created such masterpieces as the *Turquoise* and *Ukrainian Song* caskets, the panel *By the Brook* and patterned miniatures. The panel *Russia,* co-authored by N. Soloninkin, is no less striking than Gusev's experiments in shape. He and Puchkov invented a new shape of decorative painted clocks. The casket *Sixtieth Anniversary of the October Revolution* is interesting in composition: eight miniatures representing scenes from history are united by line and colour *(Soviet Rule Is Proclaimed, Civil War, Rehabilitation, World War II, Space Effort, Virgin Land, Baikal-Amur Railway* and *Soviet Constitution).*

N. Marchukov, graduate of the Fedoskino school and Moscow Artistic Design College, now teaches composition, painting and drawing in Fedoskino. He excels in townscapes *(Pskov, Novgorod, New Moscow)* and genre *(Wedding* and *Red Banner Award).* Of interest is his *Peoples' Friendship.* Interested in applied arts, Marchukov elaborated an exquisite tea service and other articles.

V. Antonov debuted in 1957 with two works, *Ivan Tsarevich and the Fire-Bird* and *Moon, Son of Moon,* the former no usual for Fedoskino and reminiscent of the Palekh school with its two-dimensional figures. Two years later, Antonov presented his *Humpback Horse,* intricate in composition and techniques, with colours in superb harmony despite the lavish gold, silver and other inlays. Unlike at the start, the artist now came back to the Fedoskino three-dimensional figures. *Hay-Making,* with its vertically elongated composition, is a glimpse back into the painter's rural childhood. The early 1970s brought us his excellent *Peasant Girl and Her Admirer* and *Troikas.* Antonov's best works include *The Red Army Enters a Village, An Evening in the Countryside, A Riverscape, The Three Maidens, Evergreen, Fedoskino in Winter* and *May Again* — this latter dedicated to the 35th anniversary of the VE-Day: a mixture of victors' triumph with mourning over the fallen heroes. Pathetic is the girl, too little to realize that Daddy will never come home. Yet life goes on, symbolized in the sunlit glade under a spreading birch-tree, where the action is laid.

Versatile and always poetic, Yu. Karapaev depicts man as one with Nature — suffice it to see his silvery *Landscape with a Willow* or the majestic *Woodland Scenery in September,* reminiscent of Strakhov's landscapes. Karapaev's fair heroines are, doubtless, girls of today, even if dressed in medieval robes, like in *The Song of the North.* The panel *Red Rowan* has an epic quality, unlike the charmingly personal *Couple, An Encounter* and *Piper.* A daring experimentor, the artist has lately produced monumental works unexpected in the Fedoskino school. *An Encounter* and *Farewell* have an inspired patriotic message. "Without losing its decorative quality, miniature painting can carry a profound social message," the artist wrote in the preface to the catalogue of his 1977 show (19).

N. Soloninkin, Lenin Komsomol Prize laureate, made portraits of World War II heroes Marshal Zhukov, General Dovator and guefrilla fighter Liza Chaikina; of cosmonauts Yuri Gagarin and Oleg Makarov, of the poet Taras Shevchenko and 17th-century military and political leader Bogdan Khmelnitsky; of 19th-century artist Savrasov, against one of his best landscapes; and of art historian Savostyanov, with deep insight into his scholarly mind and personal charm. Among Soloninkin's most ambitious efforts are the symbolical figure of a victorious soldier and the impressive Lenin portraits: *Lenin as Schoolboy, Lenin on the Rostrum, Lenin with Red Soldiers, Lenin* and *Lenin's Dream.* He also excels in genre and fairy-tale scenes, and in landscapes, be it panoramas of old fortresses and monasteries *(The Isles of Solovki)* or idyllic rural pictures, like *Ferapontovo,* an architectural landscape to which the mother-of-pearl background gives a rare decorative quality. Superb are his *Lubava, Sunflowers, Welcome, The Golden Cockerel* and *Old Peasant Couple.* In many of his works (the total number exceeds 60) Soloninkin uses intricate glazing and sfumato techniques, and decorates his miniatures with mother-of-pearl, bronze and aluminum dust, and goldleaf. An expert jeweller, he makes graceful settings for his brooch miniatures.

S. Chistov prefers genre and fairy-tale scenes, like *Humpback Horse,* full of expression and decorative beauty. *Topographer* portrays a scene from the early Soviet years. The expert, hardly demobilized from the Red Army, still in his soldiers's coat, appoints plots to be given out to peasants. A red flag is flowing on a humble hut in the background — the village greets the new life. In *Lenin Talks to Peasants,* an elderly farmer enumerates the matters for discussion on his fingers, and Lenin makes notes. Both are brought out by the masterful composition and impasto brushstrokes in smoky reds and pale gold — his favourite colour scheme. Chistov lately painted a number of interesting genre scenes from history and today's life: *The First Landplot of His Own, Off to the Army, Propagandist, Lenin, Resting, Victors* and *Builders.*

The last decade replenished the artistic community with S. Kozlov, E. Khomutinnikova, V. Smolenskaya, S. Rogatov, Jr., A. Kozlova, A. Kuznetsov, A. Fedorov and M. Rogatova — the gifted pupils of Rogatov Sr., P.S. Davydov, Larishev, Frolov and Monashov.

Kozlov's *Red Army Men* are memorable in their precise line and refined colour.

His *Town of Dmitrov*, with its sophisticated perspective, is also a thing of beauty.

Painters ever more often cooperate with jewellers. Take the fragile *Frog Princess* silver filigree box with its mother-of-pearl plaque — a fine effort by miniaturists Kozlov and Kuznetsov and jeweller Sorokin. The framing of Soloninkin's *Portrait of Cosmonaut Georgy Beregovoi* was made by jeweller Meshkov.

Khomutinnikova is best characterized by her *Tale of the Golden Cockerel,* with its original composition and radiant with humour. Smolenskaya is at her best in portraying charming young women (*At the River*). Kozlova matches her in *The Boyar Girl.*

A true professional art, Fedoskino painting is, nevertheless, close to the grassroots. Like every folk art, it is based on teamwork. So a few words now about the team, not individual painters.

Like folk songs and icons, Fedoskino masterpieces vary on the same originals, every copyist adding something all his own to eventually reach perfection. The Fedoskino method implies an original on which copyists vary in an effort taking months of nature sketching and experimenting in colour and composition — like the original work. It is a common effort of the author and copyist. They exchange their finds and arrive at the beautiful results together. It is not for nothing that copies are signed on a par with originals.

Original painters know from the start what changes this or that copyist will introduce into his figure arrangement and colour scheme. This is a true teamwork, if there ever was one.

Founded 50 years ago and headed by Mikhail Bokov for many decades, the local school trained many original painters and copyists for Fedoskino. Among the teachers are the well-known Alexander Parfenov and Ivan Vetrov.

The factory, too, has many names of enthusiastic workers to remember: Alexander Novoselsky, Roman Tatarkin and Yuri Khomutinnikov. The factory well deserves the Order of the Badge of Honour, awarded to it several years ago.

This art book presents to you close on two hundred precious masterpieces to give you an idea of a unique art, one of the best displays of Russian artistry and taste.

NOTES

(all references are to Russian editions)

[1] Ukhanova I.N. *Russian Lacquer Articles in Hermitage Collection.* Leningrad, 1964, p. 7.

[2] Ibid., p. 9.

[3] At the end of the 1820s, the Lukutin factory sold lacquer articles 2 roubles 80 kopecks to 300 roubles for a dozen, depending on the sizes and painting quality (See Ukhanova, *op. cit.,* p. 18)

[4] Bakushinsky A.V. *Studies and Essays.* Moscow, 1981, p. 269.

[5] Ibid., pp. 269-270.

[6] Ibid., p. 272.

[7] The ten founding fathers of the Fedoskino cooperative included nine Lukutin masters and one from the Vishnyakov workshops: Alexei Golovchenkov, polisher and varnisher. The rest were painters Sergei and Vasili Borodkin, Alexei Kruglikov, Ivan Lavrov, Sergei Matveyev and Vasili Mitusov; cabinet-maker Alexei Meshchaninov, varnisher Alexei Kainov and polisher Sergei Kuznetsov, elected manager.

[8] Yalovenko G.V. *Fedoskino.* Moscow, 1959, p. 36.

[9] Ibid., p. 16.

[10] Ukhanova, *op. cit.,* pp. 22-23.

[11] Yalovenko, *op. cit.,* p. 86.

[12] Gryaznov A. *The Talents of Fedoskino.* Moscow, 1970, p. 32.

[13] Ibid., p. 82.

[14] Bakushinsky, *op. cit.,* pp. 273-274.

[15] Ibid., p. 274.

[16] Ibid., p. 275.

[17] Ibid., p. 275.

[18] Yalovenko, *op. cit.,* p. 56.

[19] Yu. Karapaev. *Lacquer Painting.* Exhibition Catalogue. Foreword by N.R. Budanova. Moscow, 1977.

PLATES

1
Anonymous artist
Small box with a male portrait. Early 19th century
2
Anonymous artist
Cover with a portrait of Russian fable-writer Ivan Krylov. Mid-19th century

3
Anonymous artist
Snuff-box with a view of the Danilkovo-Fedoskino Estate. Mid-19th century
4
Anonymous artist
Snuff-box showing a peasant family. 1818-28

5
Anonymous artist
Small box with a picnic scene. 1830
6
Anonymous artist
Small box with a hunting scene. 1830

Anonymous artist
Casket with a hunting scene. 1830

8
Anonymous artist
Snuff-box showing a killed bugler. 1840
9
Anonymous artist
Cuff-link showing a peasant lad. Mid-19th century

10
Anonymous artist
Box showing a soldier on leave. 1850
11
Anonymous artist
Cuff-link showing a peasant girl. Mid-19th century

Anonymous artist
Casket with a view of the Moscow Kremlin as seen from Balchug.
Mid-19th century

Anonymous artist
Casket with a view of old Red Square.
Mid-19th century

14
Anonymous artist
Small box showing peasant women resting. Mid-19th century
15
Anonymous artist
Small box showing an elder. Late 19th century

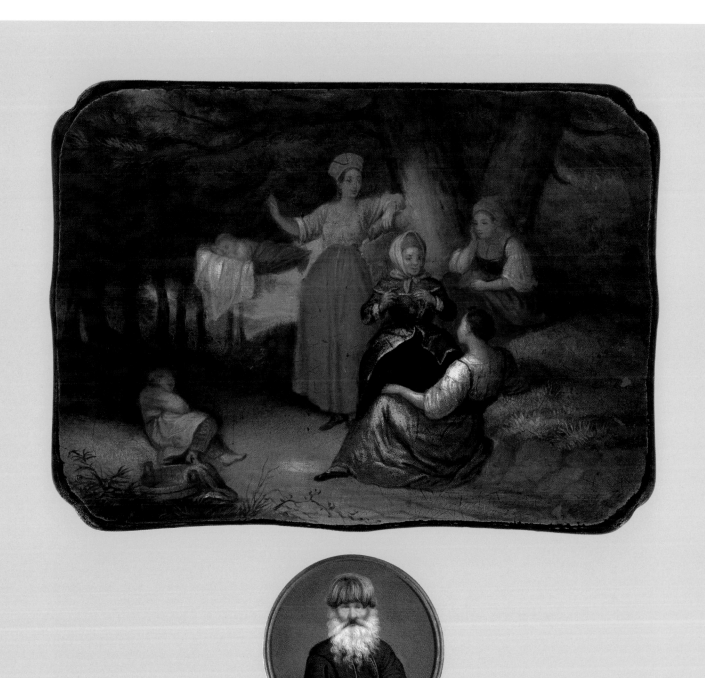

16, 17, 18
Anonymous artist
Box showing the views of Fedoskino and Russian troika coaches.
Mid-19th century

19
Anonymous artist
Cigar-case showing a peasants' dance. Mid-19th century

20
Anonymous artist
Small box showing a peasant whetting a scythe. Mid-19th century

21
Anonymous artist
Snuff-box with a hay-making scene. Mid-19th century
22
Anonymous artist
Snuff-box showing a little girl. Mid-19th century

23
Anonymous artist
Snuff-box showing a young girl. Mid-19th century

24
Anonymous artist
Small box showing a young girl. Mid-19th century

Anonymous artist
Small box with a view of Dresden. Mid-19th century

Anonymous artist
Casket with a view of St. Petersburg. Mid-19th century

Anonymous artist
Box with a scene of courting. Mid-19th century

29
Anonymous artist
Snuff-box showing peasants and a balalaika-player. Mid-19th century

30
Anonymous artist
Small box showing a hunter and a sleeping peasant girl. Mid-19th century

Anonymous artist
Box showing peasants and a young girl. Mid-19th century

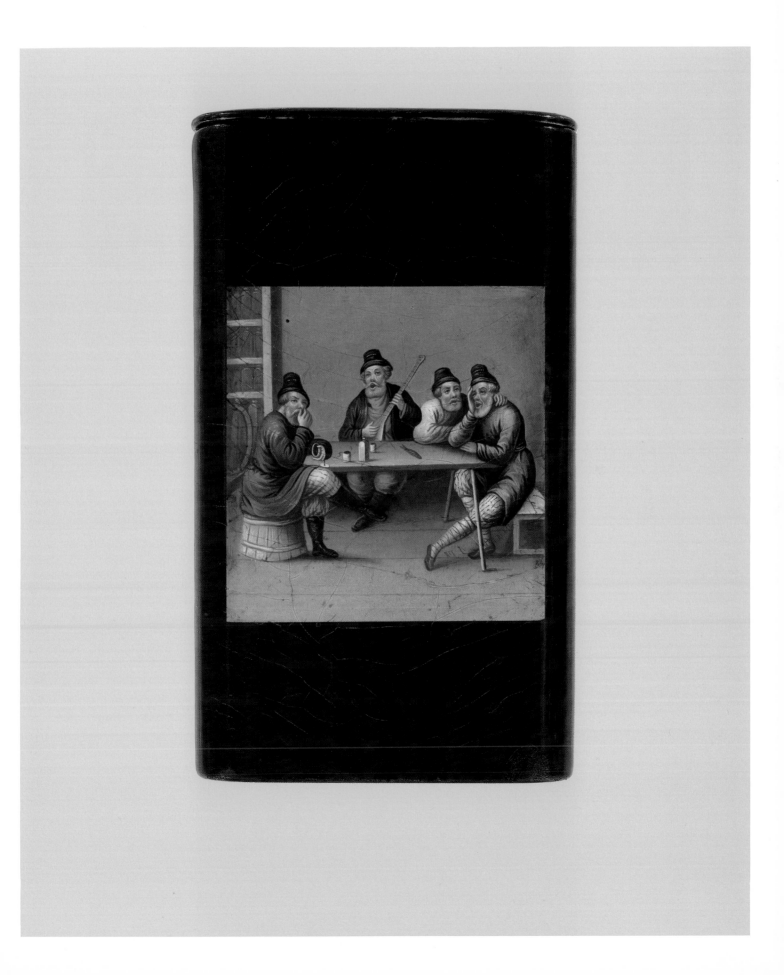

33
Anonymous artist
Glove-box decorated with a Russian troika coach. Late 19th century

34
Anonymous artist
Small box showing two peasants. Late 19th century

Anonymous artist
Cover of an album showing a peasants' dance. Mid-19th century

Anonymous artist
Cover showing a young peasant couple. Late 19th century

S. Borodkin (1850-1938)
Plaque with a Russian troika coach. Early 20th century

40
Anonymous artist
Cover with a scene after a fable by Ivan Krylov. Late 19th century
41
Anonymous artist
Small box with two peasants. 1885

Anonymous artist
Tea-caddy with a Russian troika coach. Early 20th century

43
N. Petrov (1863-1936)
Box showing a round dance. 1925

44
V. Kruglikov (1881-1947)
Casket showing a peasant girl. 1947

45
V. Borodkin (1883-1944)
Box showing a young peasant couple in the field. 1933

46
N. Tsybin (1887-1939)
Small box with a Russian troika coach. 1932

A. Kruglikov (1884-1960)
Small box showing a young coquette. Copied after V. Shtember. 1945

A. Kruglikov (1884-1960)
Casket with a view of old Moscow. 1943

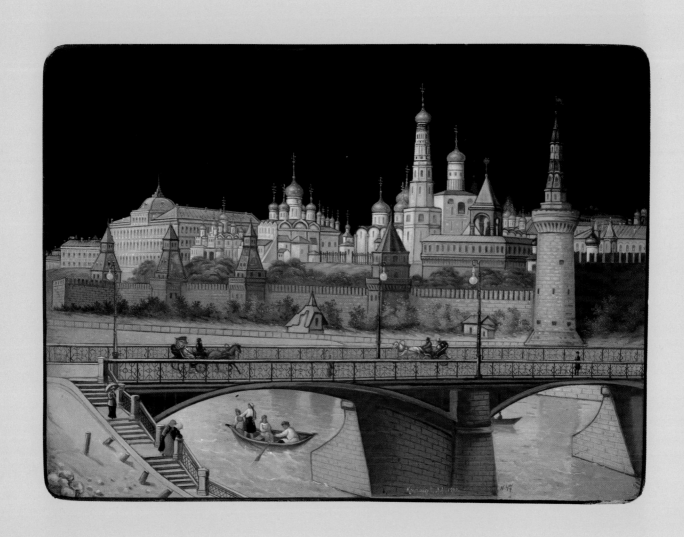

A. Kruglikov (1884-1960)
Casket with Russian troika coaches in winter-time. 1947

A. Kruglikov (1884-1960)
Casket with Russian troika coaches in summer-time. 1943

A. Kruglikov (1884-1960)
Casket showing a round dance. 1950

A. Kruglikov (1884-1960)
Casket showing holiday-makers. 1946

53
A. Kruglikov (1884-1960)
Box with a tea-drinking scene. 1956

54
I. Platonov (1887-1967)
Tea-caddy showing a ploughman in a floral cartouche. 1945

55
I. Platonov (1887-1967)
Tea-caddy decorated with a hay-making scene in a floral cartouche. 1945

56
I. Platonov (1887-1967)
Tea-caddy with a harvesting scene in a floral cartouche. 1945
57
I. Platonov (1887-1967)
Blotter showing a peasant carrying wood. 1945

M. Popenov (1889-1952)
Casket showing a peasant lad giving a present to his sweetheart. 1937

M. Popenov (1889-1952)
Casket showing mowers finishing their work. 1947

V. Lavrov (1894-1951)
Box with a tea-drinking scene. 1935

V. Lavrov (1894-1951)
Box showing an elder and a kitten. 1945

V. Lavrov (1894-1951)
Box with a tea-drinking scene. 1945

V. Lavrov (1894-1951)
Casket with a portrait of Field-Marshal Kutuzov. 1946

I. Semionov (1896-1947)
Small box showing a peasant couple. 1949

I. Semionov (1896-1947)
Box showing an accordion-player and his girl. 1930.

68
I. Semionov (1896-1947)
Casket showing a salute over the Moscow Kremlin. 1944

69
D. Orlov (born 1919)
Casket decorated with Russian troika coach in winter-time. 1949

70
A. Leznov (1886-1946)
Small barrel decorated with flowers. 1944

71
G. Tochenov (born 1917)
Box with Russian troika coaches. 1965

72
Z. Tsar (born 1918)
Box showing a young girl and a little boy frightened by a snake. 1946

73
P. Davydov (born 1919)
Box showing a bear in the sledge. 1957

74
P. Davydov (born 1919)
Small box showing Pushkin's winter outing. 1958

75
I. Strakhov (1918-1979)
Casket with a sunlit landscape. 1968

76
I. Strakhov (1918-1979)
Small box with a view of the village of Shushenskoye between 1897 and 1900. 1966

77
I. Strakhov (1918-1979)
Box with a view of an old stone bridge. 1974

78
I. Strakhov (1918-1979)
Box with a view of Fedoskino - the native land of sailor Zheleznyak. 1967

I. Strakhov (1918-1979)
Casket showing tourists. 1972

I. Strakhov (1918-1979)
Box decorated with an early spring landscape. 1972

I. Strakhov (1918-1979)
Casket with an evening riverscape. 1978

S. Rogatov (born 1920)
Large casket decorated with flowers. 1956

83
S. Rogatov (born 1920)
Panel showing a diadelphous birch-tree. 1982

84
S. Rogatov (born 1920)
Small box decorated with a summer landscape with partridges. 1959

V. Lipitsky (born 1921)
Casket showing Lel playing. 1962

V. Lipitsky (born 1921)
Small box with a Shrovetide scene. 1978

M. Rogatova (born 1962)
Box with scenes from *The Frog Princess* fairy-tale. 1989

V. Lipitsky (born 1921)
Small box showing pedlars. 1974

V. Lipitsky (born 1921)
Casket with a scene from the *Humpback Horse*. 1977

V. Lipitsky (born 1921)
Box with a portrait of Alexander Pushkin. 1977

93
V. Lipitsky (born 1921)
Casket with an illustration to the Russian fairy-tale *A Scarlet Flower*. 1979
94
M. Pashinin (born 1921)
Casket showing Lel. 1959

M. Pashinin (born 1921)
Box showing Lel and the Snow-Maiden. 1963

96
M. Pashinin (born 1921)
Small box showing Alexander Pushkin on the Neva Embankment. 1971
97
M. Pashinin (born 1921)
Small box showing the Snow-Maiden. Copied by N. Ivanov. 1959

S. Monashov (born 1923)
Case decorated with Ivan Tsarevich and the Fire-bird. 1956

99
S. Tardasov (1921-1966)
Panel with a scene from the *Humpback Horse*. 1956

100
P. Macheev (born 1921)
Small box with a view of Moscow. 1974

101
M. Korniyenko (born 1925)
Casket with a rural landscape in the evening. 1977

102
N. Balashov (born 1923)
Casket with a woodland scenery. 1975

M. Chizhov (born 1923)
Box showing children visiting Lenin. 1966

104
M. Chizhov (born 1923)
Casket showing winter festivities in Fedoskino. 1968

M. Chizhov (born 1923)
Casket with a winter scene in Fedoskino. 1963

M. Chizhov (born 1923)
Box with a winter scene at Zagorsk. 1970

107
M. Chizhov (born 1923)
Panel with a portrait of Fedoskino miniature painter A. Kruglikov. 1977
108
M. Chizhov (born 1923)
Panel with a portrait of I. Semionov, Fedoskino miniature painter. 1977

A. Sokolov (1928-1978)
Casket with a portrait of Leo Tolstoy. Copied by V. Kulgavov. 1956

110
G. Skripunov (born 1923)
Small box with a scene of a winter festival in the country. 1981.

111
G. Skripunov (born 1923)
Casket showing New Year festivities in the country. 1978

112
G. Skripunov (born 1923)
Casket with a winter scene. 1977

113
A. Tolstov (born 1929)
Casket showing peasants returning from hay-making. 1979

114
A. Tolstov (born 1929)
Small box showing a boy reading a letter to his granny. 1979

115
A. Tolstov (born 1929)
Box showing a scene of evening relaxation in the countryside. 1980
116
A. Tolstov (born 1929)
Casket with a view of the village of Fedoskino. 1979

117
G. Larishev (born 1929)
Casket showing Red horsemen in 1918. 1967

118
G. Larishev (born 1929)
Small box showing Zhostovo lacquer tray painters. 1976

119
G. Larishev (born 1929)
Box with an autumn scene. 1976

120
G. Larishev (born 1929)
Box showing a curious person. 1977

G. Larishev (born 1929)
Panel showing Ivan Tsarevich,
hero of Russian fairy-tales. 1975

G. Larishev (born 1929)
Panel showing Vasilisa the Beautiful,
heroine of Russian fairy-tales. 1975

G. Larishev (born 1929)
Casket showing the Snow-Maiden. Copied by Ye. Khomutinnikov. 1977

G. Larishev (born 1929)
Casket showing Alyonushka. 1976

125
G. Larishev (born 1929)
Small box showing mother's waiting forever. 1975

126
G. Larishev (born 1929)
Small box showing an old woman reading
her late husband's and son's letters from the front. 1975

G. Larishev (born 1929)
Casket with a view of Moscow environs during the war. 1981

G. Larishev (born 1929)
Casket with a scene from the fairy-tale *Father Frost*. 1978

G. Larishev (born 1929)
Casket showing the Magic Carpet and the Space Travel. 1979

V. Frolov (born 1931)
Panel with a tea-drinking scene. 1971

V. Frolov (born 1931)
Casket showing Russian buffoons. 1971

N. Babashko (1932-1977)
Casket with a fairy-tale scene. 1956

133
A. Kozlov (born 1932)
Casket painted with a composition
after Pushkin's *Tale of Tsar Saltan*. 1970

P. Puchkov (born 1932)
Casket with a view of Zaryadye in Moscow. 1980

135
P. Puchkov (born 1932)
Casket with a view of Red Square in Moscow
during a salute. 1979

136
P. Puchkov (born 1932)
Box with a view of the building of the Council of Ministers in Moscow. 1980
137
P. Puchkov (born 1932)
Small box with a view of the Kremlin. 1980

P. Puchkov (born 1932)
Box with a view of Luzhniki and the Novodevichi Convent in Moscow. 1981

Yu. Gusev (born 1933)
Casket with a Russian floral pattern. 1982

A. Fyodorov (born 1957)
Box showing Prince Igor's campaign. 1988

141
N. Marchukov (born 1936)
Box showing peasants gathering vegetables. 1973
142
A. Kuznetsov (born 1954)
Box with a view of Kirilo-Byelozersk Monastery. 1988

143
L. Stroganova (born 1938)
Small box showing Fedoskino women painters. 1977

144
L. Stroganova (born 1938)
Casket showing Lel. 1977

145
V. Antonov (born 1936)
Casket with a scene from the *Humpback Horse*. Copied by N. Soloninkin. 1975

146
V. Antonov (born 1936)
Panel showing Ivan Tsarevich and the Fire-bird. Copied by P. Meshchaninov. 1977

V. Antonov (born 1936)
Casket showing a peasant girl going for water and her admirer. 1972

148
V. Antonov (born 1936)
Box showing three Russian maidens. 1972

149
N. Aldoshkin (born 1931)
Small box showing a young weaver. 1976

150
Yu. Karapaev (born 1936)
Casket with a woodland scenery in September. 1974

151
Yu. Karapaev (born 1936)
Small box showing a landscape with a willow. 1980

152
Yu. Karapaev (born 1936)
Small box showing a peasant couple. 1980

153
Yu. Karapaev (born 1936)
Small box showing a peasant playing the pipe. 1979

154
Yu. Karapaev (born 1936)
Small box showing peasant girls singing a song. Copied by S. Kozlov. 1970

155
Yu. Karapaev (born 1936)
Small box showing miniature painters at Lukutin's factory. 1980

156
Yu. Karapaev (born 1936)
Small box showing a girl and a lad. 1978

N. Soloninkin (born 1945)
Panel with a portrait of pilot-cosmonaut of the USSR Georgi Beregovoi. 1985

N. Soloninkin (born 1945)
Panel with a portrait of Yuri Gagarin. 1980

159

N. Soloninkin (born 1945)
Panel with a portrait of Russian painter Alexei Savrasov. 1980

160
N. Soloninkin (born 1945)
Small box with a view of the Isles of Solovki. 1981

161
N. Soloninkin (born 1945)
Small box with a view of Ferapontovo. 1977

N. Soloninkin (born 1945)
Casket showing an old peasant couple recollecting their past. 1972

163
A. Grachov (born 1946)
Small boxes showing Tula craftsmen. 1965

164
V. Smolenskaya (born 1954)
Small box showing a girl by the waterside. 1981

S. Chistov (born 1946)
Casket with a fairy-tale scene. 1981

166
A. Kozlova (born 1958)
Casket with scenes from *Ruslan and Lyudmila*. 1989
167
S. Chistov (born 1946)
Small box showing a topographer. 1975

169
S. Kozlov (born 1955)
Box showing Red Army men playing a new march. 1980

170
S. Kozlov (born 1955)
Box with a view of the town of Dmitrov. 1978

171
S. Rogatov (born 1958)
Small box showing peasants at the fair. 1980

172
V. Golenev (born 1958)
Small box showing peasants listening to a gramophone. 1980

173
Ye. Khomutinnikova (born 1957)
Casket with a scene from *The Tale of the Golden Cockerel*. 1980
174
Ye. Khomutinnikova (born 1957)
Box showing Katiusha. 1979

175
S. Kozlov (born 1955),
A. Kuznetsov (born 1954),
V. Sorokin (born 1943)
Casket with a scene from
The Frog Princess fairy-tale. 1982

176
Fedoskino lacquerware
with ornamental painting

List of Plates

Резюме

Перечень репродукций

LIST OF PLATES

* Painted decoration in oils is worked on the papier-mâché surface of the items reproduced: every layer of paint is coated with lacquer. The measurements of the lids are given in centimetres, height before width.
The works whereabouts of which are not indicated are kept in the reserve of Fedoskino Factory of Lacquer Miniature Painting.

39. S. Borodkin. 1850-1938
Plaque with a Russian troika coach
early 20th century
*Painting and glazing over a ground
powdered with aluminum dust.
22x23*

40. Cover with a scene after a fable by
Ivan Krylov
N. Lukutin Factory, late 19th
century
*Painting over a ground powdered
with aluminum dust. 6x8*

41. Small box with two peasants
N. Lukutin Factory, 1885
Painting and glazing. 5.6x3.1x1.5

42. Tea-caddy with a Russian troika
coach
N. Lukutin Factory, early 20th
century
Painting. 9x10x8

43. N. Petrov. 1863-1936
Box showing a round dance. 1925
*Painting and glazing over a goldleaf.
11.3x16x16.3*

44. V. Kruglikov. 1881-1974
Casket showing a peasant girl. 1947
*Painting and glazing over a goldleaf.
13x9x4*

45. B. Borodkin. 1883-1944
Box showing a young peasant
couple in the field. 1933
Painting. 11x6x4

46. N. Tsybin. 1887-1939
Small box with a Russian troika
coach. 1932
*Painting over a ground powdered
with aluminum dust. 8x9x4*

47. A. Kruglikov. 1884-1960
Small box showing a young
coquette. Copied after V. Shtember
1945
*Painting and glazing over a goldleaf.
9x7x3.5*

48. A. Kruglikov. 1884-1960
Casket with a view of old Moscow.
1943
Painting. 18x22x8

49. A. Kruglikov. 1844-1960
Casket with Russian troika coaches
in wintertime. 1947
*Painting and glazing over a goldleaf
and over a ground powdered with silver dust. 18x22x8*

50. A. Kruglikov. 1884-1960
Casket with Russian troika coaches
in summer-time. 1943.
*Painting and glazing over a ground
powdered with gold dust. 18x22x8*

51. A. Kruglikov. 1884-1960
Casket showing a round dance. 1950
*Painting and glazing over gold and
silver leaves. 18x22x8*

52. A. Kruglikov. 1884-1960
Casket showing holiday-maker. 1946
Painting. 18x22x8

53. A. Kruglikov. 1884-1960
Box with a tea-drinking scene. 1956
Painting. 17x17x8

54. I. Platonov. 1887-1967
Tea-caddy showing a ploughman in
a floral cartouche. 1945
Painting. 6.8x9x7

55. I. Platonov. 1887-1967
Tea-caddy decorated with a hay-
making scene in a floral cartouche.
1945
Painting. 6.8x9x7

56. I. Platonov. 1887-1967
Tea-caddy with a harvesting scene in
a floral cartouche. 1945
Painting. 6.8x9x7

57. I. Platonov. 1887-1967
Blotter showing a peasant carrying
wood. 1945
Painting. 6.8x14

58. M. Popenov. 1889-1952
Casket showing a peasant lad giving
a present to his sweetheart. 1937
Painting. 18x18x7

59. M. Popenov. 1889-1952
Casket showing mowers finishing
their work. 1947
Painting. 18x18x7

60. V. Lavrov. 1894-1951
Box with a tea-drinking scene. 1935
Painting. 15x15x6

61. V. Lavrov. 1894-1951
Box showing an elder and a kitten.
1945
Painting. 13x13x4.5

62. V. Lavrov. 1894-1951
Box with a tea-drinking scene. 1945
Painting. 10x13x4

63. V. Lavrov. 1894-1951
Casket with a portrait of Field-
Marshal Kutuzov. 1946
Painting. 20x12x6

64. I. Semionov. 1896-1947
Small box showing a Russian troika
coach. 1934
*Painting and glazing over a ground
powdered with aluminum dust.
8x10x3*

65. I. Semionov. 1896-1947
Box showing peasants gathering
vegetables. 1939
Painting. 8x11x4

66. I. Semionov. 1896-1947
Small box showing a peasant
couple. 1949
Painting. 10x7x4

67. I. Semionov. 1896-1947
Box showing an accordion-player
and his girl. 1930
Painting. 15x8.5x4

68. I. Semionov. 1896-1947
Casket showing a salute over the
Moscow Kremlin. 1944
Painting and glazing. 15x15x8

69. D. Orlov. Born 1919
Casket decorated with Russian troika coach in winter-time, painted in
a filigree-decorated oval. 1949
Painting and glazing. 6.5x9x4.5

70. A. Leznov. 1886-1946
Small barrel decorated with
flowers. 1944
Painting. Diam. 7, height 6

71. G. Tochenov. Born 1917
Box with Russian troika coaches.
1965
*Painting and glazing over a ground
powdered with aluminum dust.
4x12x2*

72. Z. Tsar. Born 1918
Box showing a young girl and a
little boy frightened by a snake. 1946
Painting. 10.5x8x4

73. P. Davydov. Born 1919
Box showing a bear in the sledge.
1957
Painting. 12x18x4

74. P. Davydov. Born 1919
Small box showing Pushkin's winter
outing. 1958
Painting. Diam. 9, height 4

75. I. Strakhov. 1918-1979
Casket with a sunlit landscape. 1968
*Painting and glazing over a goldleaf.
18x25x6*

76. I. Strakhov. 1918-1979
Small box with a view of the Village
of Shushenskoye. 1966
*Painting and glazing over a goldleaf.
6x7.5x3.5*

77. I. Strakhov. 1919-1979
Box with a view of an old stone
bridge. 1974
*Painting and glazing over a goldleaf.
8.6x16x4*

78. I. Strakhov. 1918-1979
Box with a view of the Village of Fe-
doskino - the native land of sailor
Zheleznyak. 1967
Glazing over a goldleaf. 4x13x2

79. I. Strakhov. 1918-1979
Casket showing tourists. 1972
*Painting and glazing over a goldleaf.
22x26.5x8*

80. I. Strakhov. 1918-1979
Box decorated with an early spring
landscape. 1972
*Painting and glazing over a goldleaf.
11x17x5*

81. I. Strakhov. 1918-1979
Casket with an evening riverscape.
1989
*Painting and glazing over a ground
powdered with aluminum dust.
13x18x7*

82. S. Rogatov. Born 1920
Octahedral casket decorated with
flowers in a roundel, framed with a
floral pattern. 1956
*Painting, glazing over a mother-of-
pearl plaque; a ground powdered
with gold dust. Diam. 25, height 10.*

83. S. Rogatov. Born 1920
Panel showing a diadelphous birch-
tree. 1982
Painting. 22x30

84. S. Rogatov. Born 1920
Small box decorated with a summer
landscape with partridges, in oval.
1959
Painting 8x10x3

85. V. Lipitsky. Born 1921
Casket showing a young girl going
for water. 1978
Painting. 15.2x10.8x5

86. V. Lipitsky. Born 1921
Casket showing Lel playing. 1962
*Painting and glazing over gold and
silver leaves. 13x20x8.8*

87. V. Lipitsky. Born 1921
Small box with a Shrovetide scene.
1978
*Painting and glazing over a goldleaf;
a ground powdered with aluminum
dust. 9.5x8.2x2.5*

88. M. Rogatova. Born 1962
Box with scenes from *The Frog Prin-
cess* fairy-tale. 1989
Painting over a goldleaf. 6x5x4

89. V. Lipitsky. Born 1921
Casket showing an evening meeting.
1971
*Painting and glazing over a goldleaf.
10.5x13x2.8*

90. V. Lipitsky. Born 1921
Small box showing pedlars. 1974
Painting. 11.3x11.3x5.3

91. V. Lipitsky. Born 1921
Casket decorated with the scene
from the *Humpback Horse.* 1977
*Painting and glazing over a goldleaf.
19x25.7x9*

92. V. Lipitsky. Born 1921
Box with a portrait of Alexander
Pushkin. 1977
Painting. 11.3x11.3x5.3

93. V. Lipitsky. Born 1921
Casket with a scene from the Russian
fairy-tale *A Scarlet Flower.* 1979
*Painting and glazing over a goldleaf.
25.6x18.7x6.8*

94. M. Pashinin. Born 1921
Casket showing Lel. 1959
*Painting and glazing over a goldleaf.
13x5x4*

95. M. Pashinin. Born 1921
Box showing Lel and the Snow-
Maiden. 1963
Glazing. 12x6x4

96. M. Pashinin. Born 1921
Small box showing Alexander Pushkin on the Neva Embankment.
1971.
Painting. 6.5x4.5x2.5

97. M. Pashinin. Born 1921
Small box showing the Snow-
Maiden. 1959
Copied by N. Ivanov
Painting and glazing. 8x6x4

98. S. Monashov. Born 1923
Case decorated with Ivan Tsarevich
and the Fire-bird in oval. 1956
*Painting and glazing over a goldleaf.
6x12x4*

99. S. Tardasov. 1921-1966
Panel with a scene from the *Hump-
back Horse.* 1956
*Painting and glazing over a goldleaf.
Diam. 22.3*

100. P. Macheev. Born 1921
Small box with a view of Moscow.
1974
*Painting and glazing over a ground
powdered with bronze and aluminum dust. 3.5x10x2.5*

101. M. Korniyenko. Born 1925
Casket with a rural landscape in the
evening. 1977
Painting. 5x9x3.5

102. N. Balashov. Born 1923
Casket with a woodland scenery.
1975
*Painting and glazing over a goldleaf;
a ground powdered with aluminum
dust. 14x21x7.*

103. M. Chizhov. Born 1923
Box showing children visiting Lenin.
1966
*Painting and glazing over a goldleaf,
a ground powdered with aluminum
dust. 12x19x5*

104. M. Chizhov. Born 1923
Casket showing winter festivities in
Fedoskino. 1968
*Painting and glazing. Diam. 20,
height 7*

105. M. Chizhov. Born 1923
Casket with a winter scene at Fedo-
skino 1963.
Painting. 14x16x6

106. M. Chizhov. Born 1923
Box with a winter scene at Zagorsk.
1970
*Painting and glazing over a goldleaf.
12x15.5x5*

107. M. Chizhov. Born 1923
Panel with a portrait of Fedoskino
miniature painter A. Kruglikov. 1977
*Painting; German-silver mounting.
6.5x8.5*

108. M. Chizhov. Born 1923
Panel with a portrait of Fedoskino
miniature painter I. Semionov. 1977
*Painting; German-silver mounting.
6.5x8.5*

109. A. Sokolov. 1928-1978
Casket with a portrait of Leo Tol-
stoy. 1956
Painting. 10.5x13x5

110. G. Skripunov. Born 1923
Small box with a scene of a winter
festival in the country. 1981
Glazing over a goldleaf. 10x10x3

111. G. Skripunov. Born 1923
Casket showing New Year festivities
in the country. 1978
*Painting and glazing over a goldleaf.
8x10x5*

112. G. Skripunov. Born 1923
Casket with a winter scene. 1977
*Painting and glazing over a goldleaf.
7x10x4.2*

113. A. Tolstov. Born 1929
Casket showing peasants returning
from hay-making. 1979
*Painting and glazing over a goldleaf.
9.5x16.5*

114. A. Tolstov. Born 1929
Small box showing a boy reading a letter to his granny. 1979
Painting. 5x6.5x4.5

115. A. Tolstov. Born 1929
Box showing a scene of evening relaxation in the countryside. 1980
Painting and glazing over a goldleaf. 6.5x15.5x3.5

116. A. Tolstov. Born 1929
Casket with a view of the Village of Fedoskino. 1979
Painting and glazing over a goldleaf. 12x15x5

117. G. Larishev. Born 1929
Casket showing Red horsemen in 1918. 1967
Painting over a goldleaf. 11x26x8

118. G. Larishev. Born 1929
Small box showing Zhostovo lacquer tray painters. 1976
Painting. 7x8.5x4

119. G. Larishev. Born 1929
Box with an autumn scene. 1976
Painting and glazing over a goldleaf. 7.5x11x4

120. G. Larishev. Born 1929
Box showing a curious person. 1977
Painting. 8x11x4

121. G. Larishev. Born 1929
Panel showing Ivan Tsarevich, hero of Russian fairy-tales. 1975
Glazing over a goldleaf and a ground powdered with aluminum dust. 17x8

122. G. Larishev. Born 1929
Panel showing Vasilisa the Beautiful, heroine of Russian fairy-tales. 1975
Glazing over gold and silver leaves. 17x8

123. G. Larishev. Born 1929
Casket showing the Snow-Maiden. 1977
Copied by Ye. Khomutinnikov
Painting and glazing over gold and silver leaves. 16x20x8

124. G. Larishev. Born 1929
Casket showing Alyonushka. 1976.
Painting and glazing over gold and silver leaves. 16x20x8

125. G. Larishev. Born 1929
Small box showing mother's waiting forever. 1975
Painting. 6.5x8x3.5

126. G. Larishev. Born 1929
Small box showing an old woman reading her late husband's and son's letters from the front. 1975
Painting. 7.5x6x3

127. G. Larishev. Born 1929
Casket with a view of Moscow environs during the war. 1981
Painting over a ground powdered with aluminum dust. 18x15x6

128. G. Larishev. Born 1929
Casket with a scene from the fairytale *Father Frost*. 1978
Painting and glazing over gold and silver leaves. 14x8x5

129. G. Larishev. Born 1929
Casket showing the Magic Carpet and the Space Travel. 1979
Glazing over a mother-of-pearl plaque and goldleaf. 33x22x10

130. V. Frolov. Born 1931
Panel with a tea-drinking scene. 1971
Painting and glazing. 25x30

131. V. Frolov. Born 1931
Casket showing Russian buffoons. 1971
Painting. 18x16x3

132. N. Babashko. 1932-1977
Casket with a fairy-tale scene. 1956
Glazing over a goldleaf and over a ground powdered with aluminum dust. 18x15x6

133. A. Kozlov. Born 1932
Casket painted with a composition after Pushkin's *Tale of Tsar Saltan*. 1970
Painting and glazing over a goldleaf and mother-of-pearl plaque. 19x15.5x3.5

134. P. Puchkov. Born 1932
Casket with a view of Zaryadye in Moscow. 1980
Painting and glazing over a goldleaf and a ground gilt with bronze dust. 12x12x6

135. P. Puchkov. Born 1932
Casket with a view of Red Square in Moscow during a salute. 1979
Glazing over a goldleaf and over a ground powdered with bronze and aluminum dust. 22.7x32x10.7

136. P. Puchkov. Born 1932
Box with a view of the building of the Council of Ministers in Moscow. 1980
Painting. 6.5x15.5x3.5

137. P. Puchkov. Born 1932
Small box with a view of the Kremlin. 1980
Painting. 4x9x2.5

138. P. Puchkov. Born 1932
Box with a view of Luzhniki and the Novodevichy Convent in Moscow. 1981
Painting. 7.5x12.5x4

139. Yu. Gusev. Born 1933
Casket with a Russian floral pattern. 1982
Painting on goldleaf. 8x15.7x3.6
Property of the Russian Federation Ministry of Culture

140. A. Fyodorov. Born 1957
Box showing Prince Igor's campaign. 1988
Painting and glazing on goldleaf. 12x12x6.5

141. N. Marchukov. Born 1936
Box showing peasants gathering vegetables. 1973
Glazing. 6x13x4

142. A. Kuznetsov. Born 1954
Box with a view of Kirilo-Byelozersk Monastery. 1989
Painting and glazing over a mother-of-pearl plaque. Diam. 6, height 6

143. L. Stroganova. Born 1938
Small box showing Fedoskino women painters. 1977
Painting and glazing. 6x8x4

144. L. Stroganova. Born 1938
Casket showing Lel. 1977
Glazing over a goldleaf and mother-of-pearl plaque. 4.5x7x3

145. V. Antonov. Born 1936
Casket showing a scene from the *Humpback Horse*. 1975
Copied by N. Soloninkin.
Painting and glazing over a goldleaf. 22.7x32x10.7

146. V. Antonov. Born 1936
Panel showing Ivan Tsarevich and the Fire-bird. 1977
Copied by P. Meshchaninov.
Painting and glazing over a goldleaf; a ground powdered with aluminum dust. 35x11

147. V. Antonov. Born 1936
Casket showing a peasant girl going for water and her admirer. 1972.
Painting and glazing over a goldleaf. 14x21x7

148. V. Antonov. Born 1936
Box showing three Russian maidens. 1972
Painting and glazing over a goldleaf; a ground powdered with aluminum dust. 8x10.5x3

149. N. Aldoshkin. Born 1931
Small box showing a young weaver. 1976
Painting and glazing over a goldleaf. 8x6x3

150. Yu. Karapaev. Born 1936
Casket with a woodland scenery in September. 1974
Glazing over a goldleaf, a ground powdered with aluminum dust. 22x33x10

151. Yu. Karapaev. Born 1936
Small box showing a landscape with a willow. 1980
Glazing over a mother-of-pearl plaque. 6.5x7x3.5

152. Yu. Karapaev. Born 1936
Small box showing a peasant couple. 1980
Painting and glazing over a mother-of-pearl plaque. 10x5x3

153. Yu. Karapaev. Born 1936
Small box showing a peasant playing the pipe. 1979
Painting and glazing over a ground powdered with aluminum and bronze dust. Diam. 9.5, height 4

154. Yu. Karapaev. Born 1936
Small box showing peasant girls singing a song. 1970
Copied by S. Kozlov
Painting and glazing over a goldleaf. 7x4.5x4

155. Yu. Karapaev. Born 1936
Small box showing miniature painters at Lukutin's factory. 1980
Painting and glazing. 7.5x7x4

156. Yu. Karapaev. Born 1936
Small box showing a girl and a lad. 1978
Painting and glazing over a goldleaf. Diam. 7, height 4.5

157. N. Soloninkin. Born 1945
Panel with a portrait of pilot-cosmonaut of the USSR Georgi Beregovoi. 1985
Painting. 9.5x7. Metal framing by A. Meshkov (born 1938)

158. N. Soloninkin. Born 1945
Panel with a portrait of Yuri Gagarin. 1980
Glazing. 6.9x5.2

159. N. Soloninkin. Born 1945
Panel with a portrait of Russian painter Alexei Savrasov. 1980
Painting. 11.5x8.5

160. N. Soloninkin. Born 1945
Small box with a view of the Isles of Solovki. 1981
Glazing over mother-of-pearl plaque. 6.5x10x4.2

161. N. Soloninkin. Born 1945
Small box with a view of Ferapontovo. 1977
Glazing over a mother-of-pearl plaque: a ground powdered with bronze and aluminum dust. 4.5x6.4x2

162. N. Soloninkin. Born 1945
Casket showing an old peasant couple recollecting their past. 1972
Painting. 7.5x6x3

163. A. Grachov. Born 1946
Three small boxes showing Tula craftsmen. 1965
Painting over a goldleaf. 3x3x2 (each box)

164. V. Smolenskaya. Born 1954
Small box showing a girl by the waterside. 1981
Painting and glazing over a ground powdered with aluminum dust. 11.1x7.5x4

165. S. Chistov. Born 1946
Casket with a fairy-tale scene. 1981
Painting and glazing over a goldleaf. 13x13x5

166. A. Kozlova. Born 1958
Casket with scenes from *Ruslan and Lyudmila*. 1989
Painting and glazing over a mother-of-pearl plaque. 10x6x8

167. S. Chistov. Born 1946
Small box showing a topographer. 1975
Painting. 6x8x4

168. S. Kozlov. Born 1955
Box with a fairy-tale scene. 1977
Painting over a goldleaf. 12x10x5

169. S. Kozlov. Born 1955
Box showing Red Army men playing a new march. 1980
Glazing on goldleaf. 6.5x14.5x5

170. S. Kozlov. Born 1955
Box with a view of the town of Dmitrov. 1978
Glazing over a ground powdered with bronze and aluminum dust. 10x12x5

171. S. Rogatov. Born 1958
Small box showing peasants at the fair. 1980
Glazing over a goldleaf and ground powdered with aluminum dust. Diam. 8, height 5

172. V. Golenev. Born 1958
Small box showing peasants listening to a gramophone. 1980
Painting and glazing over a goldleaf. 7x6.5x4

173. Ye. Khomutinnikova. Born 1957
Casket with a scene from *The Tale of the Golden Cockerel*. 1980
Glazing over a goldleaf. 10x15x5

174. Ye. Khomutinnikova. Born 1957
Box showing Katiusha. 1979
Glazing over a goldleaf. 12x5.5x4

175. S. Kozlov, born 1955, A. Kuznetsov, born 1954, and V. Sorokin, born 1943
Lacquered papier-mâché casket in a silver filigree mounting, painted on a theme of the *Frog Princess* fairy tale, *glazed on a mother-of-pearl plaque. 5x7x5*

176. Fedoskino lacquerware with ornamental painting.

Illustrations in the text

I. Fedoskino Factory of Lacquer Miniature Painting awarded with the Order of the Badge of Honour. 1982.

II. Artist Alexander Gerasimov visiting lacquer miniature painters at Fedoskino. Standing, from left to right, G. Tochenov, M. Popenov, A. Novoselsky, and A. Kruglikov; seated, I. Platonov, A. Gerasimov, and Z. Tsar. *1946. Photo.*

III. Fedoskino lacquer miniature painters. From left to right, V. Nalimov, V. Lipitsky, M. Pashinin, M. Chizhov. *1982. Photo.*

IV. P. Puchkov in the workshop. *1982. Photo.*

V. In the painting workshop. *1982*

VI. Pupils of the Fedoskino School of Lacquer Miniature Painting working in the open air. *1982*

On the cover:

A. Kruglikov
Casket decorated with Russian *troika* coaches in summer. 1943
Painting and glazing over a ground powdered with gold dust. 18x22.

On the frontispiece:

V. Lipitsky
Panel showing a young girl under a birch. 1955
Painting and glazing over a goldleaf. 41x12

ЛАКОВАЯ МИНИАТЮРА ФЕДОСКИНА

Деревня Федоскино, являющаяся одним из центров современной русской лаковой миниатюры, расположена в живописных окрестностях Подмосковья на берегу реки Учи. Это старинное русское село уже около двухсот лет славится миниатюрной живописью на папье-маше. Искусство миниатюрной живописи известно в России с конца XVIII века, когда в 1795 году московский купец Петр Коробов открыл свою мастерскую в деревне Данилково, расположенной на противоположном берегу реки Учи.

В 1818 году дело перешло к родственнику Коробова Петру Лукутину и находилось во владении семьи Лукутиных 85 лет. Расписные шкатулки из Федоскина завоевали известность в России и Европе. Самым значительным владельцем фабрики был Александр Лукутин, который вместе с отцом управлял всем производством в середине XIX века. Обладая хорошим эстетическим вкусом, он придумывал для мастеров рисунки и гравюры, а его собственные сюжеты часто служили образцами для мастеров, поэтому первоначально изделия назывались лукутинскими миниатюрами и лишь позже они стали известны под именем федоскинских миниатюр.

Сам процесс изготовления лакированных изделий из папье-маше с декоративной росписью не претерпел серьезных изменений с середины девятнадцатого века.

Характерной чертой федоскинской миниатюрной живописи было сочетание корпусного письма с лессировкой по листам сусального золота, перламутровой подкладке или подкладке, покрытой металлическим порошком. Использовалась также чистая лессировка: прозрачный слой краски наносился на всю поверхность другой краски или подкладки.

В тридцатых и сороковых годах девятнадцатого века федоскинское предприятие достигло своего расцвета и до последней четверти девятнадцатого века не имело себе равных в России. Но в конце девятнадцатого века дело пошло на убыль. Лукутины закрыли свою фабрику в 1904 году, но в 1910 году десять энтузиастов построили новое здание мастерской и объединились в федоскинскую трудовую артель. После Октябрьской революции в жизни федоскинской артели, как и во всей стране, произошли коренные изменения. С каждым годом артель расширялась, и в начале двадцатых годов в ней работали такие выдающиеся живописцы, как В.М. Большаков, З.Т. Бурбышев, А.С. Семенов, Н.П. Цыбин, К.Н. Рановский, И.С. Семенов, Н.П. Петров и В.И. Лавров, которые продолжали писать традиционные тройки, чаепития и жанровые сценки. В тридцатые годы уже появилась современная трактовка этих сюжетов, художники стали проявлять интерес и к пейзажу, копировали жанровые полотна русских и советских художников. В 1931 году в Федоскине была основана школа миниатюрной живописи. К началу сороковых годов артель пополнилась выпускниками этой школы, среди них М.Г. Пашинин, В.Д. Липицкий, Г.К. Точенов, З.Л. Цар, А.С. и И.И. Страховы, С.П. Рогатов и другие. Некоторые из них в дальнейшем станут выдающимися мастерами федоскинского искусства.

В годы Великой Отечественной войны (1941-1945) большинство федоскинских мастеров сражались на фронте. В послевоенные годы, восстанавливая и развивая старую технику письма, художники создали новые образы, расширили тематику и стали обращать особое внимание на декоративность стиля и более гармоничное сочетание цветов. Создавались произведения на разнообразнейшую жанровую тематику, по мотивам художественных произведений, песен, сказок, а также историко-революционной и современной жизни. Таким образом, в кругу изящных искусств рядом со станковой живописью стоит реалистическая миниатюрная живопись на папье-маше, охватывающая все жанры.

Настоящий альбом представляет лишь часть работ федоскинских живописцев. Но даже краткое знакомство с сокровищами миниатюрной живописи Федоскина послужит приобщению к этому уникальному, национально самобытному искусству.

ПЕРЕЧЕНЬ РЕПРОДУКЦИЙ

1. Неизвестный художник
Мужской портрет
*Коробочка. Фабрика П. И. Коробова.
Начало XIX века
Папье-маше, декалькомания. Диаметр
7,5, высота 3**

2. Неизвестный художник
И. А. Крылов
*Крышка. Фабрика П. и А. Лукутиных.
Середина XIX века
Папье-маше, масло, лак, плотное
письмо. 6x4*

3. Неизвестный художник
Помещичья усадьба Данилково-Фе-
доскино
*Табакерка. Фабрика П. и А. Лукутиных.
Середина XIX века
Папье-маше, масло, лак, плотное
письмо. 5x8x4*

4. Неизвестный художник
Крестьянское семейство
*Табакерка. Фабрика П. В. Лукутина.
1818-1828
Папье-маше, масло, лак, плотное
письмо. 7,8x5,5x3,2*

5. Неизвестный художник
Пикник
*Коробочка. Фабрика П. В. Лукутина.
1830
Папье-маше, масло, лак, перламутр,
лессировочное письмо. 5,5x8,5x4,6*

6. Неизвестный художник
Охотничья сцена с собаками
*Коробочка. Фабрика П. В. Лукутина.
1830
Папье-маше, масло, лак, перламутр,
лессировочное письмо. 6x9x3*

7. Неизвестный художник
Охотничья сцена с собаками
*Шкатулка. Фабрика П. В. Лукутина.
1830
Папье-маше, масло, лак, перламутр,
сложное письмо. 15,5x20x11,3*

8. Неизвестный художник
Убитый трубач
*Табакерка. Фабрика П. В. Лукутина.
1840
Папье-маше, масло, лак, сложное
письмо. 5x8,7x3,7*

9. Неизвестный художник
Парень
*Запонка. Фабрика П. и А. Лукутиных.
Середина XIX века
Папье-маше, масло, лак, плотное
письмо. Диаметр 4,5*

10. Неизвестный художник
На побывку
*Коробка. Фабрика П. и А. Лукутиных.
1850
Папье-маше, масло, лак, плотное
письмо. 8x13x3*

11. Неизвестный художник
Девушка
*Запонка. Фабрика П. и А. Лукутиных.
Середина XIX века
Папье-маше, масло, лак, плотное
письмо. Диаметр 4,5*

12. Неизвестный художник
Кремль со стороны Балчуга
*Шкатулка. Фабрика П. и А. Лукутиных.
Середина XIX века
Папье-маше, масло, лак, плотное
письмо. 10x15x4*

13. Неизвестный художник
Старая Красная площадь
*Шкатулка. Фабрика П. и А. Лукутиных.
Середина XIX века
Папье-маше, масло, лак, плотное
письмо. 12,1x17x5,3*

14. Неизвестный художник
Отдых
*Коробочка. Фабрика П. и А. Лукутиных.
Середина XIX века
Папье-маше, масло, лак, плотное
письмо. 6x8x4*

15. Неизвестный художник
Портрет старика
*Коробочка. Фабрика Н. А. Лукутина.
Конец XIX века
Папье-маше, масло, лак, смешанное
письмо. Диаметр 5, высота 6*

16. Неизвестный художник
Село Федоскино
*Коробка. Фабрика П. и А. Лукутиных.
Середина XIX века
Папье-маше, масло, лак, золото, плот-
ное письмо. 5x20x5*

17. Неизвестный художник
Тройки
*Коробка. Фабрика П. и А. Лукутиных.
Середина XIX века
Папье-маше, масло, лак, золото, плот-
ное письмо. 5x20x5*

18. Неизвестный художник
Село Федоскино
*Коробка. Фабрика П. и А. Лукутиных.
Середина XIX века
Папье-маше, масло, лак, золото, плот-
ное письмо. 5x20x5*

19. Неизвестный художник
Крестьянская пляска
*Портсигар. Фабрика П. и А. Луку-
тиных. Середина XIX века
Папье-маше, масло, лак, смешанное
письмо. 7x10x2,5*

20. Неизвестный художник
Крестьянин, отбивающий косу
*Коробочка. Фабрика П. и А. Лукутиных.
Середина XIX века
Папье-маше, масло, лак, плотное
письмо. 8x4x3*

21. Неизвестный художник
Отдых на покосе
*Табакерка. Фабрика П. и А. Лукутиных.
Середина XIX века
Папье-маше, масло, лак, плотное
письмо. 4,9x7,6x3,1*

22. Неизвестный художник
Сидящая девочка
*Табакерка. Фабрика П. и А. Лукутиных.
Середина XIX века
Папье-маше, масло, лак, сложное лесси-
ровочное письмо. 9,5x4,3x3,2*

23. Неизвестный художник
Девушка в постели
*Табакерка. Фабрика П. и А. Лукутиных.
Середина XIX века
Папье-маше, масло, лак, перламутр, зо-
лото, сложное лессировочное письмо.
4,8x10x3,4*

24. Неизвестный художник
Девушка
*Коробочка. Фабрика П. и А. Лукутиных.
Середина XIX века
Папье-маше, масло, лак, плотное
письмо. 8x5x4*

25. Неизвестный художник
Городской пейзаж
*Табакерка. Фабрика П. и А. Лукутиных.
Середина XIX века
Папье-маше, масло, лак, плотное
письмо. 15x9x4*

26. Неизвестный художник
Вид Дрездена
*Коробочка. Фабрика П. и А. Лукутиных.
Середина XIX века
Папье-маше, масло, лак, плотное
письмо. 6x10x4*

27. Неизвестный художник
Петербург
*Шкатулка. Фабрика П. и А. Лукутиных.
Середина XIX века
Папье-маше, масло, лак, плотное
письмо. 6x10x4*

28. Неизвестный художник
Ухажер
*Коробка. Фабрика П. и А. Лукутиных.
Середина XIX века
Папье-маше, масло, лак, плотное
письмо. 15x9x4*

29. Неизвестный художник
Крестьяне, слушающие балалаечника
*Табакерка. Фабрика П. и А. Лукутиных.
Середина XIX века
Папье-маше, масло, лак, золото, плот-
ное письмо. 6,1x8x3,7*

30. Неизвестный художник
Встреча в поле
*Коробка. Фабрика П. и А. Лукутиных.
Середина XIX века
Папье-маше, масло, лак, плотное
письмо. 6x8x3*

31. Неизвестный художник
Мужики
*Коробка. Фабрика П. и А. Лукутиных.
Середина XIX века
Папье-маше, масло, лак, плотное
письмо. 7,9x13,3x2,5*

32. Неизвестный художник
Крестьяне, нюхающие табак
*Табакерка. Фабрика П. и А. Лукутиных.
Середина XIX века
Папье-маше, масло, лак, плотное
письмо. 10x7x2*

33. Неизвестный художник
Тройка
*Коробка для перчаток. Фабрика
Н. А. Лукутина. Конец XIX века
Папье-маше, масло, лак, смешанное
письмо. 12x30x10*

34. Неизвестный художник
Два мужика
*Коробочка. Фабрика Н. А. Лукутина.
Конец XIX века
Папье-маше, масло, лак, смешанное
письмо. 5,6x3,1x1,5*

35. Неизвестный художник
Крестьянская пляска
*Альбом. Фабрика П. и А. Лукутиных.
Середина XIX века
Папье-маше, масло, лак, лессировочное
письмо. 17x22,2x6*

36. Неизвестный художник
Крестьяне, слушающие балалаечника
*Пластина. Фабрика П. и А. Лукутиных.
Середина XIX века
Папье-маше, масло, лак, плотное
письмо. 16x20*

---

* Произведения, местонахождение которых не указа-
но, хранятся в фонде федоскинской ордена „Знак
Почета" фабрики миниатюрной живописи. Все раз-
меры даны в сантиметрах.

37. Неизвестный художник
Крестьяне
Крышка. Фабрика Н. А. Лукутина. Конец XIX века
Папье-маше, масло, лак, смешанное письмо. 20x20

38. Неизвестный художник
Дама и два кучера
Футляр для меню. Фабрика Н. А. Лукутина. 1890
Папье-маше, масло, лак, золото, смешанное письмо. 10,5x6,6

39. С. И. Бородкин (1850-1938)
Тройка
Пластина. Начало XX века
Папье-маше, масло, лак, алюминий, смешанное письмо. 22x23

40. Неизвестный художник
Демьянова уха
Крышка. Фабрика Н. А. Лукутина. Конец XIX века
Папье-маше, масло, лак, алюминий, плотное письмо. 6x8

41. Неизвестный художник
Два мужика
Коробочка. Фабрика Н. А. Лукутина. 1885
Папье-маше, масло, лак, смешанное письмо. 5,6x3,1x1,5

42. Неизвестный художник
Тройка
Чайница. Фабрика Н. А. Лукутина. Начало XX века
Папье-маше, масло, лак, плотное письмо. 9x10x8

43. Н. П. Петров (1863-1936)
Хоровод
Коробка. 1925
Папье-маше, масло, лак, золото, смешанное письмо. 11,3x16x6,3

44. В. А. Кругликов (1881-1947)
Девка
Шкатулка. 1947
Папье-маше, масло, лак, золото, сквозное письмо. 13x9x4

45. В. С. Бородкин (1883-1944)
Встреча в поле
Коробка. 1933
Папье-маше, масло, лак, плотное письмо. 11x6x4

46. Н. П. Цыбин (1887-1939)
Тройка
Коробочка. 1932
Папье-маше, масло, лак, алюминий, плотное письмо. 8x9x4

47. А. А. Кругликов (1884-1960)
Кокетка (копия с картины В.К. Штембера)
Коробочка. 1945
Папье-маше, масло, лак, золото, смешанное письмо. 9 x 7 x 3,5

48. А. А. Кругликов (1884-1960)
Старая Москва
Шкатулка. 1943
Папье-маше, масло, лак, плотное письмо. 18x22x8

49. А. А. Кругликов (1884-1960)
Тройки зимние
Шкатулка. 1947
Папье-маше, масло, лак, золото, серебряный порошок, смешанное письмо. 18x22x8

50. А. А. Кругликов (1884-1960)
Тройки летние
Шкатулка. 1943
Папье-маше, масло, лак, бронзовый порошок, сложное письмо. 18x22x8

51. А. А. Кругликов (1884-1960)
Хоровод
Шкатулка. 1950
Папье-маше, масло, лак, золото, серебро, смешанное письмо. 18x22x8

52. А. А. Кругликов (1884-1960)
Выходной день
Шкатулка. 1946
Папье-маше, масло, лак, плотное письмо. 18x22x8

53. А. А. Кругликов (1884-1960)
Чаепитие
Коробка. 1956
Папье-маше, масло, лак, плотное письмо. 17x17x8

54. И. А. Платонов (1887-1967)
Пахарь
Чайница. 1945
Папье-маше, масло, лак, плотное письмо. 6,8x9x7

55. И. А. Платонов (1887-1967)
На току
Чайница. 1945
Папье-маше, масло, лак, плотное письмо. 6,8x9x7

56. И. А. Платонов (1887-1967)
Жатва
Чайница. 1945
Папье-маше, масло, лак, плотное письмо. 6,8x9x7

57. И. А. Платонов (1887-1967)
Привоз дров
Пресс-папье. 1945
Папье-маше, масло, лак, плотное письмо. 6,8x14

58. М. К. Попенов (1889-1952)
Подарок
Шкатулка. 1937
Папье-маше, масло, лак, плотное письмо. 18x18x7

59. М. К. Попенов (1889-1952)
С покоса
Шкатулка. 1947
Папье-маше, масло, лак, плотное письмо. 18x18x7

60. В. И. Лавров (1894-1951)
Чаепитие
Коробка. 1935
Папье-маше, масло, лак, плотное письмо. 15x15x6

61. В. И. Лавров (1894-1951)
Стар да мал
Коробка. 1945
Папье-маше, масло, лак, плотное письмо. 13x13x4,5

62. В. И. Лавров (1894-1951)
Чаепитие
Коробка. 1945
Папье-маше, масло, лак, плотное письмо. 10x13x4

63. В. И. Лавров (1894-1951)
М. И. Кутузов
Шкатулка. 1946
Папье-маше, масло, лак, плотное письмо. 20x12x6

64. И. С. Семенов (1896-1947)
Тройка
Коробочка. 1934
Папье-маше, масло, лак, алюминий, сложное письмо. 8x10x3

65. И. С. Семенов (1896-1947)
Уборка урожая
Коробка. 1939
Папье-маше, масло, лак, плотное письмо. 8x11x4

66. И. С. Семенов (1896-1947)
Возвращение с покоса
Коробочка. 1949
Папье-маше, масло, лак, плотное письмо. 10x7x4

67. И. С. Семенов (1896-1947)
С гармошкой
Коробка. 1930
Папье-маше, масло, лак, плотное письмо. 15x8,5x4

68. И. С. Семенов (1896-1947)
Салют
Шкатулка. 1944
Папье-маше, масло, лак, смешанное письмо. 15x15x8

69. Д. М. Орлов (род. 1919)
Тройка зимняя
Ларчик. 1949
Папье-маше, масло, лак, смешанное письмо. 6,5x9x4,5

70. А. И. Лезнов (1886-1946)
Цветы
Бочонок. 1944
Папье-маше, масло, лак, плотное письмо. Диаметр 7, высота 6

71. Г. К. Точенов (род. 1917)
Тройки
Коробка. 1965
Папье-маше, масло, лак, алюминий, смешанное письмо. 4x12x2

72. З. Л. Цар (род. 1918)
Испугались змеи
Коробка. 1946
Папье-маше, масло, лак, плотное письмо. 10,5x8x4

73. П. Н. Давыдов (род. 1919)
Генерал Топтыгин
Коробка. 1957
Папье-маше, масло, лак, плотное письмо. 12x18x4

74. П. Н. Давыдов (род. 1919)
А. С. Пушкин на прогулке
Коробочка. 1958
Папье-маше, масло, лак, плотное письмо. Диаметр 9, высота 4

75. И. И. Страхов (1918-1979)
Солнечный луч
Шкатулка. 1968
Папье-маше, масло, лак, золото, смешанное письмо. 18x25x6

76. И. И. Страхов (1918-1979)
В далеком Шушенском. 1897-1900 гг.
Коробочка. 1966
Папье-маше, масло, лак, золото, смешанное письмо. 6x7,5x3,5

77. И. И. Страхов (1918-1979)
Старый мостик
Коробка. 1974
Папье-маше, масло, лак, золото, смешанное письмо. 8,6x16x4

78. И. И. Страхов (1918-1979)
Федоскино — родина матроса
Железняка
Коробка. 1967
Папье-маше, масло, лак, золото, сложное лессировочное письмо. 4х13х2

79. И. И. Страхов (1918-1979)
Туристскими тропами
Шкатулка. 1972
Папье-маше, масло, лак, золото, смешанное письмо. 22х26,5х8

80. И. И. Страхов (1918-1979)
К весне
Коробка. 1972
Папье-маше, масло, лак, золото, смешанное письмо. 11х17х5

81. И. И. Страхов (1918-1979)
Вечер на Уче
Шкатулка. 1978
Папье-маше, масло, лак, алюминий, смешанное письмо. 13х18х7

82. С. П. Рогатов (род. 1920)
Цветы
Ларец. 1956
Папье-маше, масло, лак, перламутр, золото, смешанное письмо. Диаметр 25, высота 10

83. С. П. Рогатов (род. 1920)
Березка
Панно. 1982
Папье-маше, масло, лак, плотное письмо. 22х30

84. С. П. Рогатов (род. 1920)
Летний пейзаж. Куропатки
Коробочка. 1959
Папье-маше, масло, лак, плотное письмо. 8х10х3

85. В. Д. Липицкий (род. 1921)
По улице мостовой
Шкатулка. 1978
Папье-маше, масло, лак, плотное письмо. 15,2х10,8х5

86. В. Д. Липицкий (род. 1921)
Песня Леля
Ларец. 1962
Папье-маше, масло, лак, золото, серебро, сложное письмо. 13х20х8,8

87. В. Д. Липицкий (род. 1921)
Масленица
Коробочка. 1978
Папье-маше, масло, лак, золото, алюминий, смешанное письмо. 9,5х8,2х2,5

88. М.С. Рогатова (род. 1962)
Сказка о Царевне-лягушке
Коробка. 1989
Папье-маше, масло, лак, золото, плотное письмо. 6х5х4

89. В. Д. Липицкий (род. 1921)
Вечерком
Шкатулка. 1971
Папье-маше, масло, лак, золото, смешанное письмо. 10,5х13х2,8

90. В. Д. Липицкий (род. 1921)
Коробейники
Коробка. 1974
Папье-маше, масло, лак, плотное письмо. 11,3х11,3х5,3

91. В. Д. Липицкий (род. 1921)
Конек-Горбунок
Ларец. 1977
Папье-маше, масло, лак, золото, смешанное письмо. 19х25,7х9

92. В. Д. Липицкий (род. 1921)
А. С. Пушкин
Коробка. 1977
Папье-маше, масло, лак, плотное письмо. 11,3х11,3х5,3

93. В. Д. Липицкий (род. 1921)
Аленький цветочек
Шкатулка. 1979
Папье-маше, масло, лак, золото, смешанное письмо. 25,6х18,7х6,8

94. М. Г. Пашинин (род. 1921)
Лель
Шкатулка. 1959
Папье-маше, масло, лак, золото, смешанное письмо. 13х5х4

95. М. Г. Пашинин (род. 1921)
Лель и Снегурочка
Коробка. 1963
Папье-маше, масло, лак, лессировочное письмо. 12х6х4

96. М. Г. Пашинин (род. 1921)
А. С. Пушкин
Коробочка. 1971
Папье-маше, масло, лак, плотное письмо. 6,5х4,5х2,5

97. М. Г. Пашинин (род. 1921)
Снегурочка. Копия (художник-исполнитель Н. В. Иванов)
Коробочка. 1959
Папье-маше, масло, лак, смешанное письмо. 8х6х4

98. С. В. Монашов (род. 1923)
Жар-птица
Баул. 1956
Папье-маше, масло, лак, золото, сложное лессировочное письмо. 6х12х4

99. С. Н. Тардасов (1921-1966)
Конек-Горбунок
Панно. 1956
Папье-маше, масло, лак, золото, смешанное письмо. Диаметр 22,3

100. П. Н. Мачеев (род. 1921)
Вид Москвы
Коробочка. 1974
Папье-маше, масло, лак, бронза, алюминий, смешанное письмо. 3,5х10х2,5

101. М. И. Корниенко (род. 1925)
Вечерний пейзаж
Шкатулка. 1977
Папье-маше, масло, лак, плотное письмо. 5х9х3,5

102. Н. И. Балашов (род. 1923)
Пейзаж
Шкатулка. 1975
Папье-маше, масло, лак, алюминий, золото, смешанное письмо. 14х21х7

103. М. С. Чижов (род. 1923)
В гости к В. И. Ленину
Коробка. 1966
Папье-маше, масло, лак, золото, алюминий, смешанное письмо. 12х19х5

104. М. С. Чижов (род. 1923)
Праздник зимы в Федоскине
Шкатулка. 1968
Папье-маше, масло, лак, смешанное письмо. Диаметр 20, высота 7

105. М. С. Чижов (род. 1923)
Федоскино
Шкатулка. 1963
Папье-маше, масло, лак, плотное письмо. 14х16х6

106. М. С. Чижов (род. 1923)
Зима в Загорске
Коробка. 1970
Папье-маше, масло, лак, золото, смешанное письмо. 12х15,5х5

107. М. С. Чижов (род. 1923)
Портрет А. А. Кругликова
Панно. 1977
Папье-маше, масло, лак, мельхиор, плотное письмо. 6,5х8,5

108. М. С. Чижов (род. 1923)
Портрет И. С. Семенова
Панно. 1977
Папье-маше, масло, лак, мельхиор, плотное письмо. 6,5х8,5

109. А. С. Соколов (1928-1978)
Л. Н. Толстой. Копия (художник-исполнитель В. С. Кульгавов)
Шкатулка. 1956
Папье-маше, масло, лак, плотное письмо. 10,5х13х5

110. Г. В. Скрипунов (род. 1923)
Праздник
Коробочка. 1981
Папье-маше, масло, лак, золото, сложное лессировочное письмо. 10х10х3

111. Г. В. Скрипунов (род. 1923)
Новый год
Шкатулка. 1978
Папье-маше, масло, лак, золото, смешанное письмо. 8х10х5

112. Г. В. Скрипунов (род. 1923)
Зима
Шкатулка. 1977
Папье-маше, масло, лак, золото, смешанное письмо. 7х10х4,2

113. А. А. Толстов (род. 1929)
Возвращение с покоса
Шкатулка. 1979
Папье-маше, масло, лак, залото, смешанное письмо. 9,5х16х5

114. А. А. Толстов (род. 1929)
Письмо
Коробочка. 1979
Папье-маше, масло, лак, плотное письмо. 5х6,5х4,5

115. А. А. Толстов (род. 1929)
Вечер в деревне
Коробка. 1980
Папье-маше, масло, лак, золото, смешанное письмо. 6,5х15,5х3,5

116. А. А. Толстов (род. 1929)
Моя деревня
Шкатулка. 1979
Папье-маше, масло, лак, золото, смешанное письмо. 12х15х5

117. Г. И. Ларишев (род. 1929)
За власть Советов
Шкатулка. 1967
Папье-маше, масло, лак, золото, плотное письмо. 11х26х8

118. Г. И. Ларишев (род. 1929)
Жостовские мастера
Коробочка. 1976
Папье-маше, масло, лак, плотное письмо. 7х8,5х4

119. Г. И. Ларишев (род. 1929)
Осень
Коробка. 1976
Папье-маше, масло, лак, золото, смешанное письмо. 7,5х11х4

120. Г. И. Ларишев (род. 1929)
Любопытный
Коробка. 1977
Папье-маше, масло, лак, плотное письмо. 8x11x4

121. Г. И. Ларишев (род. 1929)
Иван-царевич
Панно. 1975
Папье-маше, масло, лак, золото, алюминий, сложное лессировочное письмо. 17x8

122. Г. И. Ларишев (род. 1929)
Василиса Прекрасная
Панно. 1975
Папье-маше, масло, лак, золото, серебро, сложное лессировочное письмо. 17x8

123. Г. И. Ларишев (род. 1929)
Снегурочка. Копия (художник-исполнитель Е. Ю. Хомутинникова)
Шкатулка. 1977
Папье-маше, масло, лак, золото, серебро, смешанное письмо. 16x20x8

124. Г. И. Ларишев (род. 1929)
Аленушка
Шкатулка. 1976
Папье-маше, масло, лак, золото, серебро, смешанное письмо. 16x20x8

125. Г. И. Ларишев (род. 1929)
Вечное ожидание
Коробочка. 1975
Папье-маше, масло, лак, плотное письмо. 6,5x8x3,5

126. Г. И. Ларишев (род. 1929)
Старые фронтовые письма
Коробочка. 1975
Папье-маше, масло, лак, плотное письмо. 7,5x6x3

127. Г. И. Ларишев (род. 1929)
Подмосковье
Шкатулка. 1981
Папье-маше, масло, лак, алюминий, плотное письмо. 18x15x6

128. Г. И. Ларишев (род. 1929)
Морозко
Шкатулка. 1978
Папье-маше, масло, лак, золото, серебро, смешанное письмо. 14x8x5

129. Г. И. Ларишев (род. 1929)
От сказки к были
Ларец. 1979
Папье-маше, масло, лак, перламутр, золото, сложное лессировочное письмо. 33x22x10

130. В. Н. Фролов (род. 1931)
За столом. Чаепитие
Панно. 1971
Папье-маше, масло, лак, смешанное письмо. 25x30

131. В. Н. Фролов (род. 1931)
Скоморохи
Шкатулка. 1971
Папье-маше, масло, лак, плотное письмо. 18x16x3

132. Н. М. Бабашко (1932-1977)
Сказка
Шкатулка. 1956
Папье-маше, масло, лак, золото, алюминий, сложное лессировочное письмо. 18x15x6

133. А. И. Козлов (род. 1932)
Сказка о царе Салтане
Ларец. 1970
Папье-маше, масло, лак, золото, перламутр, сложное письмо. 19x15,5x3,5

134. П. Н. Пучков (род. 1932)
Москва. Зарядье
Шкатулка. 1980
Папье-маше, масло, лак, золото, бронза, алюминий, смешанное письмо. 12x12x6

135. П. Н. Пучков (род. 1932)
Салют
Ларец. 1979
Папье-маше, масло, лак, алюминий, блонза, золото, сложное лессировочное письмо. 22,7x32x10,7

136. П. Н. Пучков (род. 1932)
Москва. Вид на здание Совета Министров РСФСР
Коробка. 1980
Папье-маше, масло, лак, плотное письмо. 6,5x15,5x3,5

137. П. Н. Пучков (род. 1932)
Вид на Кремль
Коробочка. 1980
Папье-маше, масло, лак, плотное письмо. 4x9x2,5

138. П. Н. Пучков (род. 1932)
Лужники
Коробка. 1981
Папье-маше, масло, лак, плотное письмо. 7,5x12,5x4

139. Ю. В. Гусев (род. 1933)
Русский узор
Шкатулка. 1982
Папье-маше, масло, лак, золото, сложное письмо. 8x15,7x3,6
Министерство культуры РСФСР

140. А.А. Федоров (род. 1957)
Поход князя Игоря
Коробка. 1988
Папье-маше, масло, лак, золото, смешанное лессировочное письмо. 12x12x6,5

141. Н. Г. Марчуков (род. 1936)
Уборка урожая
Коробка. 1973
Папье-маше, масло, лак, смешанное лессировочное письмо. 6x13x4

142. А.В. Кузнецов (род. 1954)
Кирилло-Белозерский монастырь
Коробка круглая. 1988
Папье-маше, масло, лак, перламутр, смешанное письмо. Диаметр - 6, высота - 6

143. Л. А. Строганова (род. 1938)
Мастера
Коробочка. 1977
Папье-маше, масло, лак, золото, смешанное письмо. 6x8x4

144. Л. А. Строганова (род. 1938)
Лель
Шкатулка. 1977
Папье-маше, масло, лак, перламутр, золото, сложное лессировочное письмо. 4,5x7x3

145. В. Д. Антонов (род. 1936)
Конек-Горбунок. Копия (художник-исполнитель Н. М. Солонинкин)
Ларец. 1975
Папье-маше, масло, лак, золото, смешанное письмо. 22,7x32x10,7

146. В. Д. Антонов (род. 1936)
Жар-птица. Копия (художник-исполнитель П. И. Мещанинов)
Панно. 1977
Папье-маше, масло, лак, золото, алюминий, смешанное письмо. 35x11

147. В. Д. Антонов (род. 1936)
Вдоль по улице
Шкатулка. 1972
Папье-маше, масло, лак, золото, смешанное письмо. 14x21x7

148. В. Д. Антонов (род. 1936)
Три девицы
Коробка. 1972
Папье-маше, масло, лак, золото, алюминий, смешанное письмо. 8x10,5x3

149. Н. П. Алдошкин (род. 1931)
Пряха
Коробочка. 1976
Папье-маше, масло, лак, золото, смешанное письмо. 8x6x3

150. Ю. В. Карапаев (род. 1936)
Сентябрь
Ларец. 1974
Папье-маше, масло, лак, золото, алюминий, сложное лессировочное письмо. 22x33x10

151. Ю. В. Карапаев (род. 1936)
Пейзаж с ивой
Коробочка. 1980
Папье-маше, масло, лак, перламутр, сложное лессировочное письмо. 6,5x7x3,5

152. Ю. В. Карапаев (род. 1936)
Парочка
Коробочка. 1980
Папье-маше, масло, лак, перламутр, смешанное письмо. 10x5x3

153. Ю. В. Карапаев (род. 1936)
Мелодия
Коробочка. 1979
Папье-маше, масло, лак, бронза, алюминий, смешанное письмо. Диаметр 9,5, высота 4

154. Ю. В. Карапаев (род. 1936)
Северная песня. Копия (художник-исполнитель С. И. Козлов)
Коробочка. 1970
Папье-маше, масло, лак, золото, смешанное письмо. 7x4,5x4

155. Ю. В. Карапаев (род. 1936)
Лукутинские мастера
Коробочка. 1980
Папье-маше, масло, лак, смешанное письмо. 7,5x7x4

156. Ю. В. Карапаев (род. 1936)
Встреча
Коробочка. 1978
Папье-маше, масло, лак, золото, смешанное письмо. Диаметр 7, высота 4,5

157. Н.М. Солонинкин (род. 1945)
Портрет космонавта Г.Т. Берегового
Пластина. 1985
Папье-маше, масло, лак, плотное письмо. 9,5x7. Металлическое обрамление А.Н. Мешкова

158. Н. М. Солонинкин (род. 1945)
Портрет Юрия Гагарина
Панно. 1980
Папье-маше, масло, лак, сложное лессировочное письмо. 6,9x5,2

159. Н. М. Солонинкин (род. 1945)
Портрет А. К. Саврасова
Панно. 1980
Папье-маше, масло, лак, плотное письмо. 11,5x8,5

160. Н. М. Солонинкин (род. 1945)
Соловки
Коробочка. 1981
Папье-маше, масло, лак, перламутр, сложное лессировочное письмо. 6,5x10x4,2